THE FARM JOURNAL BOOK OF WESTERN HORSEMANSHIP

Saddle Up!

THE FARM JOURNAL BOOK OF WESTERN HORSEMANSHIP

Saddle Up!

by

CHARLES E. BALL

J. B. LIPPINCOTT COMPANY

Philadelphia and New York

Copyright © 1970 by Farm Journal, Inc.
All rights reserved
Second Printing
Manufactured in the United States of America
Library of Congress Catalog Card No.: 71-110653

All photos are by Charles E. Ball except as follows: Figure 2, Bill Crump;
3, Gray's Studio; 9, Shel Hershorn; 11, Johnny Johnson; 12, Alexander; 13,
H. D. Dolcater; 23–29, 31, 33, Gary & Clark; 32, Mary Ann Ball; 54, Jane
Fallaw.

Contents

Contents

Introduction

Everybody is talking about horses—about the return of the horse, the horse population explosion, the amazing new horse industry, the thrill of owning a horse.

And for good reasons. For centuries, the horse has been a faithful servant of man, helping him win wars, till the soil and conquer the West. More recently, we have seen the horse as a friend of youth (from six to sixty), as a developer of skills, sportsmanship, discipline, confidence, responsibility, pride and personal recognition—things that all young people yearn for and need.

As a 4-H Club leader—our thirty-five members all have horses in the City of Dallas—I have discovered that no other project equals the horse in getting a kid's attention and holding it. Our 4-H objective is the development of youth, in citizenship and leadership rather than just in horsemanship, and the horse has proved an excellent means toward that end.

Another remarkable thing about horses and the way they are used today—they become a family project. Our horses have done more to bring our family together than anything that has ever happened.

Many people apparently have discovered the same thing. For horses make up the fastest growing project in the 4-H Clubs across the country. The number of 4-H'ers with horses has jumped from 37,531 in 1959 to more than 230,000 today, and the number is still climbing.

In addition, there are saddle clubs, rodeo clubs, riding stables or breeding farms popping up in nearly every city, community or county of the United States. Not only for youngsters but for doctors, lawyers, farmers, secretaries, housewives and other adults.

Horses are a status symbol today. Not a symbol of a mobile society, as they once were in the West, but a symbol of relief from a mechanized society. Horses help people unwind.

Horse numbers are increasing, too. From a peak of 25,742,000 in 1920, the horse and mule population dwindled to 2,955,000 in 1959, the last year that the U.S. Census reported them. But the U.S. Department of Agriculture (USDA) estimates that we now have nearly 7 million horses and predicts 10 million by 1977, when approximately 82 million people are expected to ride a horse at least once a year!

For all these people—horsemen and those who want to be horsemen—this how-to-do-it book is written. Most of the earlier books on horsemanship have been on English riding, because this (especially dressage) has been considered one of the performing arts for centuries. But most of the interest today is in Western riding—where the action is!

Although I have owned and ridden horses most of my life, I wanted to make this book as authoritative and helpful to serious horsemen as possible. So in addition to visiting professional trainers from coast to coast, I engaged two top trainers as consultants: L. N. Sikes and Darrell Davidson.

Mr. Sikes is a former trick horse trainer, a national rodeo performer, professional roper and trainer of many champion horses. He now operates a stable at Van Alstyne, Texas, where he specializes in training roping horses and cutting horses and in helping young horsemen.

Mr. Davidson, who trained horses in Oklahoma most of his life, is a riding instructor and operates a training stable at Dallas, Texas. He has taught many boys, girls, men and women to ride, then fitted them with winning horses. Also, he is an adult leader of a 4-H Horse Club.

The information in this book should help you in buying a horse that fits you, in training him properly, in showing him to win and in having many happy, safe hours of riding.

—CHARLES E. BALL

THE FARM JOURNAL BOOK OF WESTERN HORSEMANSHIP

Saddle Up!

1.
Before You Buy a Horse

"There is a horse for every rider, but not every horse fits every rider." That saying, told to me by a sage old horseman years ago, is as true today as it was then.

Owning a good horse can be one of the most exciting and satisfying experiences of your life. He can become a safe and loyal companion, responsive to your treatment and training, proficient and persevering in competitive events, a mirror of his master's mood and personality (Figure 1).

1. A horse becomes a mirror of his master's mood and personality. If the horse fits the rider, he will be a safe and loyal companion.

2. *A family affair. "If Father and Mother don't ride, they usually end up as groom and water boy," says the author, at left.*

But this doesn't always happen. One of the unfortunate things I have seen—many times—is for a boy or girl to fall in love with a horse that "doesn't fit." It is even worse when parents go out and pay big money for a young, untrained horse for a young, inexperienced rider and expect great things from them. These things often lead to frustrations and unhappiness—just the opposite of what you bought a horse for—and sometimes to mishaps or serious accidents. But they can be avoided, if you don't act in a hurry and if you seek reliable counsel *before you buy a horse*.

12

3. Horses are making a rapid comeback, for relaxed riding and as a competitive sport. They're popular with boys and girls from six to sixty, but girl riders outnumber boy riders by three to one.

4. Horses are the fastest-growing 4-H Club project. No other animal responds more to love, care and training. Thus horses help teach responsibility, agility and sportsmanship.

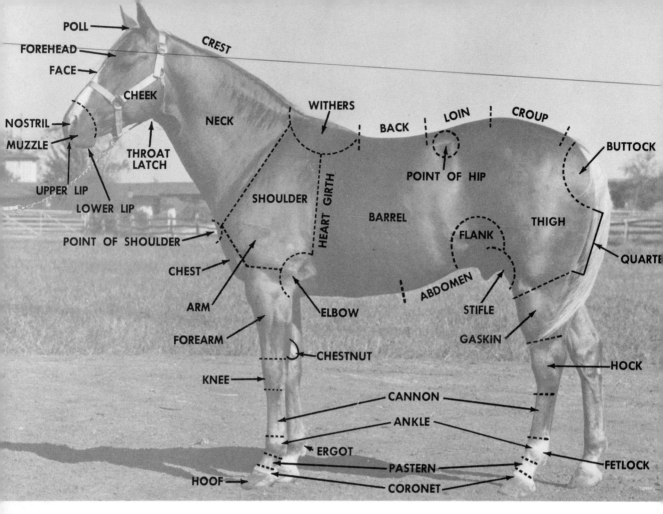

5. *The parts of a horse. Learn them so you can talk like a horseman, communicate with your veterinarian and evaluate horses better.*

How, then, should you go about selecting and buying a horse? First, if you are a beginner, you should read up on horses. Learn the parts of a horse (Figure 5) and some horse terms (Chapter 12) so you can talk knowledgeably and not get the "horsehair pulled over your eyes." Also, you should learn something about breeds and their characteristics. With horses, experience is the best teacher. But reading helps.

The next step is to decide what you want to do with your horse—learn to ride, show at Western pleasure, show at halter or race in timed events. Few horses are outstanding at all of these; if so, they usually are very expensive.

Then you must decide how big a horse you want, what age and sex,

14

what breed, how much you can afford to pay and, finally, where to get help in buying him.

SIZE, AGE AND SEX

The size of a horse is measured in hands (a hand is 4 inches, about the width of a man's hand) from the top of his withers to the ground (Figure 6). A horse 60 inches tall would be 15 hands tall. A 14.2-hand horse is 14 hands and 2 inches tall, not $14\frac{2}{10}$ hands.

A pony is a horse under 14.2 hands (Figure 7). Of course, you don't want a horse so big that the rider looks lost or out of control; but neither does a child necessarily need a small pony. Ponies, so small that they never have been ridden by an adult horseman, often are spoiled and hard to handle. They may even become mean, after learning that they can outsmart the child rider.

6. The author measures a horse for James Davidson, one of his 4-H Club members. The height of a horse is measured in 4-inch hands, from the ground to the withers.

7. Some small riders, like Gail Phillips, prefer small horses, like Joker, 10 hands tall. But ponies that are too small to have been ridden by an adult can be spoiled and hard to handle.

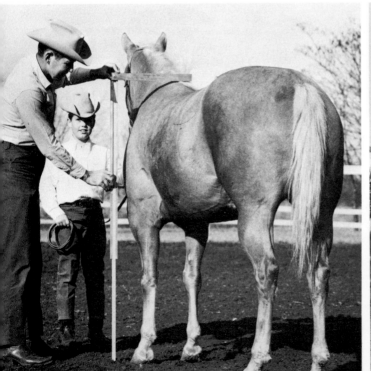

How about age and sex? Don't overlook an old horse—they are most in demand these days. As a friend quipped recently, "If I could find enough old, trained horses, I could get rich."

One year in a horse's life is equal to about three and a half years for a person. If well cared for, most horses are useful for about twenty years. But a three-year-old, which is half colt and half horse, is kind of like a teen-age boy—steady at times but unpredictable at other times.

It's expecting too much of a kid to learn to ride and to train a young horse at the same time. Buying an old horse is the better approach. When Bill Ray, Texas county agent who has helped many 4-H Club members with horses, needed a horse for his six-year-old daughter, he bought an eighteen-year-old mare (Figure 8). "It was the best three-hundred-dollar purchase we ever made," he says. "This horse was professionally trained, several kids had learned to ride on her, and Elizabeth is learning a lot from the horse."

8. Beginning riders need an old horse. Six-year-old Elizabeth Ray learned much from eighteen-year-old Miss Majo, a professionally trained Quarter Horse.

9. *Everybody admires a colt. But not everybody needs one. Most boys and girls don't have adequate facilities for raising a colt, which means it may get cut or hurt.*

Girls have a tendency to fall in love with a horse (more so than boys) and never want to sell him, even when they want a new horse. "But the more different horses you can ride the more you will learn," says Blair Smith, California horseman and judge. "So plan on stepping up as you advance, plan on owning more horses, and you'll be much happier."

On the sex of their horse, girls often prefer mares, "Because I hope to raise a colt." But most girls (and boys) don't have the facilities for raising colts (Figure 9). And if you don't have good facilities—good pasture, good fences and a good building—don't try it. I've been down that road several times and lost more colts or had them permanently injured than I've raised to maturity.

Some trainers think mares are more intelligent than geldings (castrated males); but once a month, for two or three days during their heat period, mares may be harder to handle. A gelding usually is more settled and more dependable at all times than a mare or a stallion. Stallions definitely are not safe for children or amateur horsemen.

17

10. *The Quarter Horse is named for his amazing speed over short distances, such as quarter-mile races, and can be used in many other sporting events. This horse is Otoe, one of the top Quarter Horse stallions.*

WHICH BREED FOR YOU?

True horsemen admire a good horse, regardless of breed. And there are good horses in every breed. So buy a horse of the breed that you like best or will serve your needs best. Here are a few of the more popular breeds among Western riders.

The Quarter Horse (Figure 10) is the most popular breed of all today, because he is an action horse capable of performing in many ways—pleasure riding, reining, barrel racing, roping, cutting, racing and ranch work, to name a few. Also, most Quarter Horses are intelligent and have a good disposition, traits that are preferred by cowboys and amateur riders alike.

This is a young breed; the first Quarter Horse (Wimpy, bred by the King Ranch) was registered in 1941. But this type of horse dates back to the colonial era, three hundred years ago, when match racing was the leading outdoor sport in the Carolinas and Virginia. The name Quarter Horse comes from his amazing burst of speed for short distances (official races are 440 yards or a quarter mile), which requires heavy muscling and agility.

Although you find more Quarter Horses in the Southwest and West, where they are used to work cattle, they are growing in popularity in all areas, particularly in the Midwest and East.

The Appaloosa (Figure 11), a colorful breed, was developed by the Nez Percé tribe of American Indians from about 1730 to 1830. However, ancient art portrays spotted horses with similar markings before recorded history. No two Appaloosas have identical markings. Most have a blanket of white over the loin and hips with dark round or egg-shaped spots. Some carry this marking over their entire body. They are widely used for working stock and in parades, rodeos, shows, racing and drill teams.

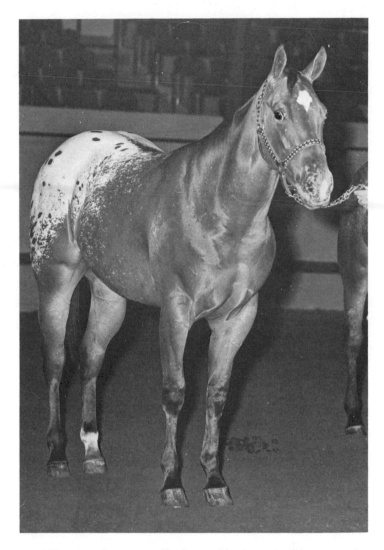

11. The Appaloosa usually has a blanket of white over the loin and hips. All have white circles around the eyes and skin that is mottled with black and white spotting, but no two Appaloosas have identical markings. This is Snowcap's Lady Pitt.

12. The Arabian, represented here by Laureate, has been called the aristocrat of horses. Note his arched neck, high tail, convex forehead, dished face and nearly level croup.

The Arabian (Figure 12), the oldest breed of horse, has been used to develop and improve all other breeds. It is believed to be a descendant of the wild Libyan horse of north Africa, which became domesticated in Egypt and got to Arabia by way of Palestine sometime between the first and sixth centuries.

Because of his intelligent-looking head, arched neck, high tail and gay way of going, the Arabian often is called the aristocrat of horses. Other distinguishing characteristics are his convex forehead, dished face and nearly level croup. Purebred Arabians are much in demand these

*13. The Paint or Pinto, intro-
duced by Spanish conquistadores,
is a color breed, either dark with
white spots, as here, or white with
dark spots. This is Yellow Mount,
the first APHA champion.*

days for showing, pleasure riding and parades. Because of their endurance and intelligence, they make good stock horses, too.

The Paint or Pinto horse (Figure 13), brought into the United States
by Spanish conquistadores, is a color breed that soon became a favorite
of the Indians. There are two basic patterns: *overo,* where the primary
color is dark (bay, brown, black, dun, sorrel or roan) with white spots
or an irregular pattern, and *tobiana,* where white is the primary color
with a secondary dark color. Glass or blue eyes are common among
Paints or Pintos.

The Palomino horse, also of Spanish extraction, is selected primarily for color, but three associations now register them as a color breed. The ideal Palomino color is that of a newly minted gold coin (but may be slightly lighter or darker) with mane and tail that is white, silver or ivory. This flashy color has made them popular, especially with women and children, for parade and pleasure riding. Also, they are used as stock horses and fine harness horses.

The Morgan horse, known for his stamina and versatility, is popular as a pleasure horse, especially in New England, where he is shown in both Western and English show classes. With a crested neck, short back and muscular body, the Morgan gives the appearance of a very strong and rather heavy horse for his size. Most Morgans are 14.1 to 15.1 hands high, weighing 900 to 1,100 pounds. All Morgan horses trace back to a little bay stallion owned by Justin Morgan of Vermont in the 1890's. He lived for thirty-two years and is said to have outrun, outpulled and out-trotted all challengers.

COSTS

How much does a horse cost? Of course, this depends on the breed, bloodline, section of the country, quality of the horse and degree of training. In the Southwest and West, grade or unregistered horses start at around $200 and go up to about $500, if well trained. Registered Quarter Horses, without training, vary from about $300 to $1,000, depending on bloodlines.

Trained horses are worth more, of course, depending on how well they have turned out. A $300 young horse with $300 worth of professional training usually will bring you more pleasure and satisfaction than a $1,000 young horse without training. Professional training usually costs $100 to $150 per month and is a good investment, especially if you start with a young horse.

The average horse owner in the United States spends $735 per year on his mount, estimates Dixon D. Hubbard, Extension animal scientist for the USDA. Of course, these expenses would be much smaller on farms and larger in or near cities where there is no pasture. But only 40 percent of the current population of 7 million horses is on farms.

FINDING HELP

When you are ready to go horse hunting, *be sure to get the help of a professional or an experienced horseman.* Horses vary as much as people, and you can't always tell their character or behavior by just looking. Some horses are temperamental, others are stable; some are fast and excitable, others are slow and calm; some are intelligent and eager to learn, others are dumb and lazy. An experienced horseman can recognize these traits and select the horse that fits you on the basis of your temperament, your size, your skill and your plans.

Beware of horse auctions or strange traders. The auctions are for pros—and the gullible! It's easy for a slick trader to tranquilize a bronc or doctor up an unsound horse so that he looks good during a sale. "If you are buying from a trader, without the help of an experienced horseman, talk to people who have bought from him before," advises L. N. Sikes, who has trained and traded over a thousand horses. "Some traders have a reputation for selling unsound horses and not standing behind them. Yet others are anxious to fit the horse and rider, and will stand behind them."

When looking at a new horse, it's easy to get emotional and see only his good points. But after the novelty wears off, you may find a lot of things wrong with him. Your best bet is to ride the horse several times or, preferably, take him home with you for a week or two to try out. But not all sellers, even some with good horses, are that accommodating.

It's also wise to have a veterinarian examine the horse. A $15 or $25 vet bill now may save you lots of money and sadness later. And if the horse is sound, the seller won't object at all.

After checking for the common unsoundnesses, the vet should observe the horse in the stall for stall vices, like cribbing, weaving or stable walking; examine his eyes for problems, teeth for age, ears for hearing defects; check the horse's lungs with a stethoscope and his circulatory system by noting heartbeat and pulse before exercise; and examine the reproductive organs.

Then the horse should be worked, so the vet can check any traveling or gait faults and recheck the horse's lungs, heart and pulse rates after vigorous exercise. And during the entire examination, he should take note of the horse's character, temperament and disposition.

Of course, you want to guard against unsoundnesses, but don't worry too much about blemishes (scars, rope burns, saddle marks, etc.). They may detract from the horse's appearance but will not affect his serviceability.

2.
Care of Your Horse

A beautiful, sleek, well-performing horse is no accident. He usually is developed by a proud owner—an owner who sees that he is fed properly and who follows a regular health program, grooms him faithfully, gives careful attention to the feet and follows good management in general.

PROPER FEEDING

Horse nutrition can be an involved subject. If you are breeding horses or raising colts, you may want to learn how to balance a ration and figure out the least-cost rations. If so, a number of good bulletins and booklets on nutrition are available from your county agent or feed manufacturer.

But a good feeding program doesn't have to be involved or complicated. In fact, a simple ration is best for most young horsemen. So let's just discuss a practical feeding program for the adult horse, its cost, and some feeding tips.

In considering what feeds to use, keep in mind that you must supply your horse with the following:

1. *Carbohydrates* for energy, to maintain the horse's body heat and supply fuel to power the muscles—for walking, heartbeat, breathing, blinking eyes and the like.

2. *Protein,* which forms the greater part of the muscles, internal organs, skin, hair coat, etc.

3. *Minerals,* which are necessary for strong bones (about 5 percent of the horse's weight), sound teeth and proper functioning of the blood.

4. *Vitamins,* which are small in amount but necessary for growth, reproduction, milk production and general health.

5. *Water,* which is about 50 percent of the body weight and must be replenished daily. It's the cooling system, acts as a lubricant and is necessary for most of the chemical functions. The average horse will drink eight to twelve gallons of water a day.

Okay, how much you should feed? This varies with each horse, depending on his size, how much work he is doing, how much feed he wastes and his "doing ability." Some horses are "good doers" (efficient feed converters) while others are "rawbones."

The most important thing is to watch your horse's condition and adjust his feed accordingly. Observe his weight, general appearance, hair coat and alertness. If you're still unsure, ask a trainer or experienced horseman to look him over and appraise your feeding program.

For the average horse, Dr. W. M. Beeson, well-known nutritionist at Purdue University, suggests the following amount of feed:

1. An idle horse or one ridden only once or twice a week can maintain himself on a good grass pasture in the spring, summer and early fall. But during winter or long periods of drouth, you'll need to supplement the pasture with a little grain or hay and maybe a protein supplement (linseed meal, soybean meal, cottonseed meal or alfalfa pellets).

2. For light work, allow about ½ pound of grain and 1¼ to 1½ pounds of hay per day per 100 pounds of body weight, plus 1 pound of protein supplement.

3. For medium work, feed 1 pound of grain and 1 to 1¼ pounds of hay per day per 100 pounds of body weight, plus 1 pound of protein supplement.

4. For heavy work, up the amount to 1¼ to 1½ pounds of grain

and 1 pound of hay per day per 100 pounds of body weight, plus 1 pound of protein supplement.

So an average thousand-pound horse doing medium work (four to five hours a day) should get about 9 pounds of grain and 10 to 12 pounds of hay, plus 1 pound of protein supplement. Also, your horse should never be without salt, preferably *loose salt* fed free choice.

Most horsemen think in terms of gallons or quarts, rather than pounds, so you should weigh your feed occasionally (Figure 14). In general, a quart of oats will weigh 1 pound, a quart of barley 1½ pounds, a quart of shelled corn 1¾ pounds. A bale of hay usually weighs 45 to 60 pounds.

14. Bill and James Davidson weigh feed.

What kinds of grain and hay are best? Horses adore oats, and oats are good for them. Because oats are more fibrous than other grains, they can be fed without much danger of hurting the horse. However, if you can't buy oats at a reasonable price, you can substitute corn, grain sorghum, wheat or barley (all should be coarsely ground). Many horsemen like to feed half oats and half corn or grain sorghum.

Timothy is the most popular hay among old-time horsemen. But there are other good hays, such as alfalfa (it contains more minerals and vitamins), legume hay, prairie hay or coastal Bermuda. The most important thing is that your hay be free of dust and mold, which can give the horse colic or heaves. (The heaves come from inhaling dust.)

Many professional trainers feed a simple ration of four parts oats, one part wheat bran (a laxative), and alfalfa hay. In fact, a lot of champions have been produced on this ration.

When buying all their feed, members of our 4-H Club in Dallas have found that commercial horse and mule feeds are just as economical as grain. And when formulated by a reputable feed manufacturer, they contain a proper balance of all nutrients. When preparing for shows, however, some of our members will add 1 pound of linseed meal a day, or 1 to 2 pounds of a protein supplement, or 2 ounces of a mineral-vitamin mixture, or a honey-based conditioner. For only 10 to 30 cents per day, this assures their horse of bloom and a glossy hair coat—makes him look like a champion!

In the city, where hay storage is sometimes a problem, some horse owners have gone to all-in-one pellets (also called cubes or checkers), which most feed companies now sell. They contain roughage, grain and a balance of all the other nutrients needed—all in one pellet. Although a little more expensive, the pellets are more convenient.

Now, how much does it cost to feed a horse properly? If you haven't learned it by now, you'll find that a horse is expensive! A mistake that some kids and inexperienced parents make is to buy a $150 or $200 horse and think their expenses are over. Not so!

15. Sawdust makes excellent bedding. Straw and sand also are good. If you pick up the droppings daily and completely replace the bedding weekly, you'll have fewer flies and your horse will be comfortable.

If you feed a horse the recommended amounts of grain, hay and supplements, and buy all the feed at retail prices, it'll cost you 75 cents to $1.00 a day. Add the boarding cost (a minimum of $10 per month), veterinary supplies and services (a minimum of $25 per year) and you're up to $425 a year, at least. And some folks spend twice that much.

Then there is bedding, if your horse is kept in a stall (Figure 15). Whatever the bedding material—straw, wood shavings, sawdust or sand —it should be three to six inches deep. The stall should be "picked" (droppings picked up with a fork) each day and the bedding completely replaced once a week or when it becomes dirty.

Scientists at the University of Connecticut recently studied the costs and merits of various types of bedding. When the stall was cleaned three times a week and the materials purchased by the ton, the costs ran like this: $20.28 per year for sand, $34.84 per year for straw and $42.12 per year for sawdust. Their conclusion: Sand requires good drainage and is less comfortable to horses; straw requires more labor in cleaning the stalls; sawdust, if available, is the most practical bedding material to use.

Here are ten tips on feeding and management that will help you and your horse:

1. Feed your horse regularly, about the same time each day. If working him, feed twice a day but never just before or just after work.

2. Keep the doors to your feed room locked. More horses founder from overeating than starve.

3. If it is necessary to change your feeding program, do it gradually—over a period of days—to avoid upsetting your horse's digestive system.

4. Throw away any grain or feed that is moldy or spoiled. It can make your horse sick.

5. Feed hay that is free of dust. If stuck with dusty hay, sprinkle it with water and feed immediately.

6. If your horse is nervous and spills his ration, feed in a larger manger which catches the spilled ration.

7. Don't feed by hand. It encourages nibbling, which can lead to nipping. Feed in a trough or bucket.

8. Provide plenty of fresh clean water, but do not let your horse drink much when hot. On trail rides or at shows, water him two or three times a day.

9. Keep a constant supply of loose salt for your horse, fed free choice.

10. Adjust the feed as necessary, according to your horse's condition, hair coat and alertness.

GOOD GROOMING

Your horse will enjoy being thoroughly groomed. It not only gives him a shiny hair coat but gentles him and conditions the skin and muscles for better performance. A true horseman will try to groom his horse every day.

The basic tools for grooming (Figure 16) are: (1) a rubber currycomb, (2) a metal currycomb (for removing mud only), (3) a dandy or coarse bristle brush, (4) a body or fine bristle brush, (5) a grooming cloth, preferably of wool, (6) a hoof pick or screwdriver for cleaning hoofs, (7) a mane and tail comb and (8) clippers or scissors for trimming the mane and fetlocks (Figure 17).

16. Some system is needed for keeping up with grooming equipment, such as the box in front of Mary Ann Ball. Basic tools include a rubber currycomb, coarse bristle brush, fine bristle brush, wool grooming cloth, hoof pick, and tail and mane comb; more if you are showing.

17. Your horse needs a haircut every month. Heavy clippers like these cost $50 to $70.

Once you have the equipment, you will need some system to keep up with it, especially if you are traveling to shows. Some young horsemen use a bucket but I prefer a box with a place for everything and everything in its place. If you carry extra supplies to the show—water bucket, water can, sponge rag, shoe polish or hoof dressing, fly repellent, show halter, chaps, spurs, registration papers, etc.—you'll find that a check list inside the box will save time and get you there with everything.

When grooming, I suggest you follow a regular order of work. One good procedure is to start at the head and work back on the near side, including the feet and legs. Then go to the off side and work back. Be gentle around the head and lower parts of the legs, because there is no fat or muscle in these areas to cushion the hard edges of the currycomb. Use only a soft brush or cloth around the head.

18. A rubber curry-comb is easier on your horse and better, unless you have mud to remove. Rub in a circular motion, then brush off the loose dirt and dust with a brush.

The rubber currycomb (Figure 18) should be used in circular motions. Next, follow with the coarse brush, then the soft brush, and finish with the grooming cloth.

Never be in such a hurry to ride that you forget to clean your horse's feet; this is a part of grooming, too. Clean the hoof from the heel to toe (Figure 19), paying particular attention to the area around the frog, which is the triangular pad in the sole of the horse's foot. (See Chapter 3 for the proper way to pick up a horse's foot.)

Most horses need their feet trimmed about every six weeks. For a horse running in pasture and working only on soft roads, shoes usually are not necessary. But if you are showing regularly or if your horse has bad feet in any way, metal shoes will help him.

19. Remember to clean your horses's feet. Using a hoof pick or screwdriver, clean from the heel to the toe, carefully removing rocks and mud around the frog.

20. If you bathe your horse, use shampoo or a soft soap.

Many horsemen bathe their horses; others only wash the feet, tail and mane. A bath does no harm, if you use a soft soap and rinse well (Figure 20). However, the soap removes most of the natural oil from the hair coat; if you are preparing for a show, bathe your horse several days ahead so that his coat will be shiny by show time.

Keeping Your Horse Healthy

It's easier and far better to *keep* your horse in top condition than to attempt to correct a problem after it becomes serious. Either way, you are sure to need the services of a veterinarian sooner or later, so I suggest that you get acquainted with a veterinarian and let him help you plan a health program *before* you have a problem.

Recommended health programs will vary a little over the country, because some diseases and parasites are worse in certain areas than in others. But as a basic program, W. M. Romane, Doctor of Veterinary Medicine at Texas A & M University, suggests regular injections for these four common diseases:

1. For *strangles* or *distemper,* most common among young horses, three weekly injections the first year followed by an annual booster until the horse is five years old.

2. For *encephalomyelitis* or *sleeping sickness,* two injections each summer, seven to fourteen days apart, for horses of all ages.

3. For *equine influenza,* two injections each fall, six to twelve days apart, for horses of all ages.

4. For *tetanus* or *lockjaw,* two injections the first year, four to eight weeks apart, followed by a booster shot each year thereafter.

There are fifty-seven species of internal parasites that have been found inside horses, according to S. L. Kalison, Doctor of Veterinary Medicine at Virginia Polytechnic Institute. But the three that cause the most trouble are: *strongyles* (blood-sucking worms that penetrate the intestines and attach to small blood vessels); *ascarids* (roundworms that penetrate the intestinal wall, enter the bloodstream and are carried to the liver and lungs); and *bots* (larvae of botflies whose eggs, laid on the horse's hair, are licked off by the horse and make their way to the stomach).

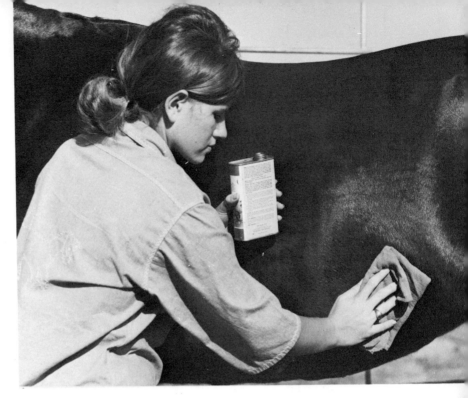

21. Because her horse shies from a spray, Bettie Massey wipes on insecticide with a rag, to control flies. Storing the damp rag in a sealed coffee can conserves insecticide.

To control these, Dr. Kalison suggests a minimum of two treatments (spring and fall) and up to six treatments if the problem persists, as indicated by fecal examination. Several drugs can be used; your veterinarian will know which ones are best. Drenching with a stomach tube (by your veterinarian) is the best way to worm a horse, but mixing the drugs with the feed, if directions are followed closely, is better than nothing. Powders and capsules also can be used.

It is impossible to eliminate all internal parasites, but Dr. Kalison says these additional steps will help: (1) keep the stalls clean and dry, (2) dispose of manure by composting or spreading on ungrazed areas, (3) mow pastures and drag the droppings with a chain harrow frequently and (4) do not overstock pastures and rotate them as frequently as possible. The drug treatments should be used in addition to these management procedures, not in place of them.

If your horse is to be comfortable and healthy, you also must control external parasites, such as flies, lice and mites. Here's a control program that works for many horsemen:

Flies. Spray or sponge the horse daily with one of the good insecticides (Figure 21). Also, occasionally spray the walls and ceiling of the stall;

22. *A sweet fly bait also is effective and easy to use. Bill Davidson sprinkles bait on wet feed sack, out of reach of horse.*

but remove the horse for this and do not contaminate the feed or water. Baits are effective, too, and often are more convenient (Figure 22).

Lice. These insects, both biting and sucking kinds, are seen most often in the winter and spring on poorly groomed horses with long hair. They cause horses to rub and patches of bare skin show up. To control, spray or sponge with chlordane (spray only), Co-Ral, Delnav or toxaphene and repeat again in two or three weeks.

Mites. Often called mange, these insects cause itching, loss of hair and crusty or folding skin. A good treatment is to brush briskly with a liquid concentration of 0.6 percent lindane or 0.5 percent toxaphene; then repeat once a week until the trouble disappears.

3.
Basic Horsemanship

No horse can be a pleasure, no horse can be a good investment, unless he is a safe horse. Furthermore, no horse is safe unless the rider uses some horse sense and follows some basic rules of horsemanship.

HOW TO CATCH A HORSE

Let's start in the beginning—with catching your horse. Maybe I'm lucky, but of the last ten or twelve horses I've owned none has been difficult to catch. Kids that seem to have the most trouble often have spoiled the horse, or maybe a previous owner did.

In a stall, always make your horse turn and face you. If he turns his heels toward you, scold him or swat him with your halter.

If he is in a pasture with other horses that like to run, you may have a problem. In this case I would use feed to catch him or try to get them all into a catch pen and isolate my horse. Using feed to catch a horse is all right, but once you start doing this you will probably have to continue it.

Occasionally, I see a boy or girl chasing his horse. How foolish! I know no boy or girl that can outrun a horse. In a lot or catch pen, if you stand still, the horse usually will become inquisitive and come to you. Or he'll stop and face you so you can approach him (Figure 23).

After catching a horse, I always take time to reward him, usually by petting or rubbing him. In some cases, I feed him, especially if he is kept in a pasture.

23. To catch a horse, don't rush and don't chase him. If you stand still, he'll usually come to you; or he'll stand for you to approach him.

How to Halter and Tie a Horse

I like to approach the horse with the halter open and in position to slip onto his head (Figures 23 and 24). By putting my right arm over

24. *To halter the horse, have your halter open and in position to slip on his head. With my arm over his neck and my hip against his shoulder, I can hold him. Hold the lead rope with a finger or lay it over your arm, in case it's suddenly needed.*

his neck and my hip against his shoulder, he isn't likely to get away. If you are too small to halter this way, however, you might want to slip the lead rope around his neck first so he won't get away. Then reward him with some kind words and gentle strokes.

25. To lead the horse, walk beside his neck, holding the lead rope near the halter, and push forward. Never get out in front and try to pull him. The loose end of rope is gathered in my left hand.

To lead him, walk along beside his neck (Figure 25) and push forward on the lead rope. This is safer, because you always have an eye on him, and the horse will lead better than if you are out in front trying to drag him.

Now you're ready to tie your horse and groom him. When tieing, I always use a strong lead rope—never tie with bridle reins—and tie him securely to a post, tree or other sturdy object. Never tie to a weak board

26. *Tie a horse with the halter and a strong lead rope. I like to tie them high and close to a sturdy object so there's no danger of his foot getting over the rope.*

or wire fence, because a horse can pull it loose, and you never want him to get the habit of breaking loose when tied. Also, I like to tie the horse high and close (Figure 26).

Tieing your horse low and long, so he can graze, is not doing him a favor. My daughter did this at a recent show, thinking Koko would enjoy the nearby grass. But Koko got his foot over the rope, burned his pastern and had a sore foot for a month.

How to Saddle and Bridle

To saddle a horse, I first lay the blanket well up on his withers and drag it back five or six inches to stroke the hairs back. Then I make sure the blanket has no wrinkles. For heavy riding, I usually put a hair pad under the blanket; some horsemen prefer to have a wool blanket next to their horse and place a pad between folds of the blanket.

Next, I pull the girths and right stirrup over the seat of the saddle and ease the saddle onto the horse's back (Figure 27), trying not to disarrange or wrinkle the blanket. Then I reach under the pommel and pull up the blanket a little to make sure it isn't binding on his withers.

27. To saddle, lay the girths and right stirrup over the seat. Then gently set the saddle on the horse's back without disarranging the blanket.

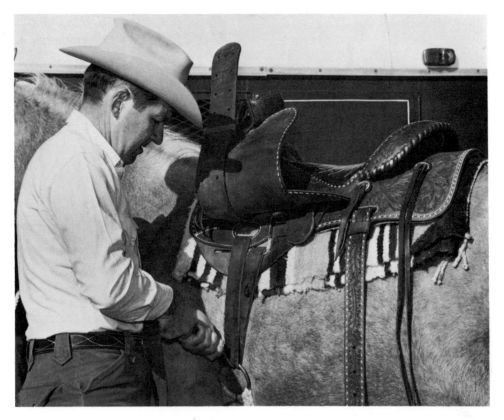

28. To tighten cinch strap or latigo, hang the left stirrup over the saddle horn. If the horse swells up, pull it reasonably tight, then walk him in a small circle and tighten it another notch or two.

Now I'm ready to cinch the horse (Figure 28). If his skin wrinkles under the girth or if he tends to swell up, I move his left front foot forward with my toe. Another way to get rid of the wrinkles is to pick up his left front foot and pull it forward 60 to 90 degrees. Then I lead him around in a circle for a few steps, until he quits swelling, and tighten the cinch strap another hole or two.

49

29. *Last step in saddling is to fasten the flank girth. I like it to touch or almost touch the horse's belly. A very loose flank girth serves no purpose.*

The last step in saddling is to fasten the flank girth (Figure 29). I like it to touch or almost touch the horse's belly. If you let the flank girth swing down three or four inches, as so many amateur riders do, you're better off without it.

By the way, when unsaddling, loosening the flank girth is the *first step*. Once I forgot to do this and attempted to take the saddle off with the flank girth still connected. With the saddle dangling under his belly, my old pony—perfectly gentle, I thought—began bucking and practically ruined a new saddle.

You know how to carry a saddle the easy way? Lots of folks have been riding for years and don't know. Fold the girths and stirrups over the seat, place the pommel on your hip, hold on to the cantle and it's easy (Figure 30).

30. To carry a saddle, fold the girths and stirrups over the seat, place the pommel on your hip and hold onto the cantle. To set a saddle on the ground, stand it on end on the saddle blanket.

31. The proper way to bridle a horse: With halter around his neck, hold the headstall with your right hand between his ears. Use fingers of your left hand to hold the curb strap out of the way and guide the mouthpiece between his teeth. Note that reins are lying over my arm, rather than dangling on the ground.

After my horse is saddled, I bridle him. The reason for bridling last is that I want him tied for saddling and, remember, you always tie a horse with a halter and strong lead rope, never with the bridle reins.

To bridle a horse, I slip the halter back on his neck and fasten it so he isn't completely free, in case he refuses to be bridled. Then I hold the headstall with my right hand between his ears and hold the bit with my left hand (Figure 31). With my fingers, I can pull the curb strap back out of the way and guide the mouthpiece between his teeth. If he doesn't open readily, I slip my thumb into the side of his mouth, where there are no teeth, and press it open, thus making room for the bit.

Never grab the shank of the bit and try to force the mouthpiece between his teeth, because you're apt to hurt his gums and make him harder than ever to bridle.

How to Pick up a Horse's Foot

Every horseman should know how to pick up a horse's foot—safely. In fact, you should get in the habit of checking and cleaning your horse's feet every time you ride him.

The proper way to pick up his left front foot, for example, is to stand just in front of his foot. Place your left hand on his shoulder and run your right hand down his leg to the cannon or fetlock. Then push on his shoulder with your left hand or with your shoulder, shifting his weight to his off foot, and pull up on the fetlock (Figure 32).

32. To pick up the horse's left front foot: (A) Place your left hand on his shoulder and run your right hand down his leg to cannon or fetlock. (B) Push with your left hand or left shoulder (shifting his weight to the off foot) and pick up the foot.

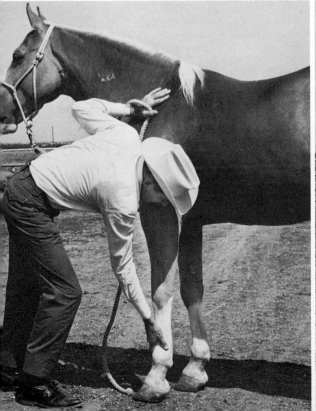
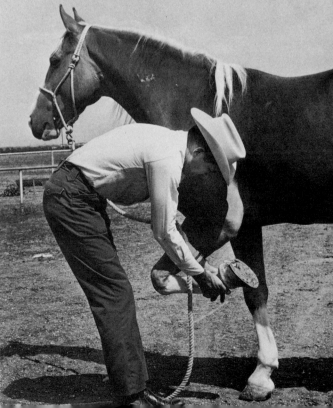

Another way, which is safe enough with gentle horses, is to run your left hand down his left leg and pinch the leaders behind his cannon with your fingers until he picks up the foot.

Picking up his hind foot is almost as easy and safe, if done properly.

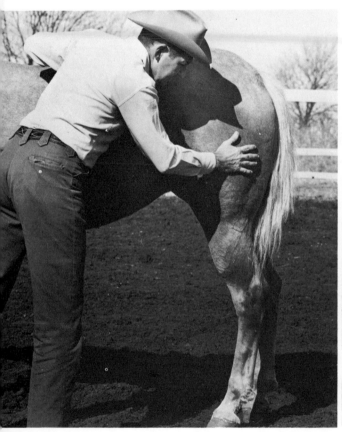

33. *To pick up the hind foot: (A) With your left hand on the horse's hip, run your right hand down his leg to the cannon. (B) Pull the leg forward, bending it at the hock. (C) Walk straight back, resting his cannon on your thigh. (D) Lock your arm over his hock, and he isn't likely to kick.*

With your left hand on his hip, run your right hand down his leg to the cannon. Pull it forward and upward, bending his leg at the hock. Then walk straight back, resting his cannon on your thigh, until your arm is locked over his hock (Figure 33).

HORSE SENSE VS. NONSENSE

As we said earlier, no horse is a pleasure unless he is safe and unless he is ridden safely. Most of the accidents that I know about have been with gentle horses. And nearly all have been the fault of the human, not the horse. A few examples:

—The woman visiting our 4-H Club pasture who walked up, unannounced, behind a horse that was eating. Lots of horses will kick when they're eating. She suffered a broken jaw and ended up with eight false teeth.

—Our neighbor who walked into a closed trailer, leading his horse right behind. The horse jumped in (a well trained horse), crushed the man and broke his nose. (For safe loading, see Chapter 10, "Trailers and Trailering.")

—The two girls who were racing their horses outside our arena during a horse show. Because of the congestion, one girl ran into a third horse, killed it and broke the third rider's leg.

—The man I know who walked up behind his young horse and swatted him on the rump without alerting the beast. This was a professional trainer who knew better, but he was talking to a friend and forgot. The result: a smashed face.

—And then there was the impatient horseman who couldn't get his nag to square up, while practicing for a halter class, and kicked the horse on the shin. I ended up with a broken big toe!

Here are some DO's and DON'Ts that will help you have fun with horses—*safely:*

DO approach a horse from his left, saddle from his left and mount from his left. This is a tradition that dates back to the knights who carried big swords on the left side and found it easier to throw their right leg over the saddle.

DON'T walk up behind a horse unannounced. Let him know you are approaching by speaking to him and placing your hand on him. Horses can't see immediately behind them and instinctively kick to protect their blind spot.

DO keep your hands calm and your voice quiet. Shouting or beating an excited horse will only make matters worse.

DON'T wrap the lead rope or reins around your hand, wrist or body. The gentlest horse sometimes spooks.

DO walk beside your horse when leading him—not in front of him— and grasp the lead rope near the halter or the reins near the bit.

DON'T tie your horse with the bridle reins. Use a strong halter and lead rope to tie him high and close to a post or tree or similar object.

DO slow to a walk when riding on pavement, bridges, ice or anywhere you're not sure of the footing.

DON'T mount your horse in a barn or near fences. It's a good way to get your head cracked or your leg cut.

DO check your girth, cinch straps, curb chain and reins to make sure they are in good condition.

DON'T tease your horse or let him nibble on you. A nibbling horse occasionally bites.

DO keep your head clear when bridling a horse. He may throw his head to avoid the bit and hit you.

4.
Training the Young Horse

There probably are as many successful ways to train horses as there are to raise children. I have seen several top professional trainers use different techniques and each end up with a champion.

This section on training the young horse will be abbreviated, because I firmly believe that, in general, training is a job for the pros. "Everybody is entitled to ruin one horse," says my son Chuck, who teaches horsemanship at a summer camp. And I assure you, he and I ruined our share before we learned our limitations.

The good trainers have spent years studying horses; it's their business. They understand the mind of a horse, his temperament, senses, behavior and reactions to varying situations. They even recognize and can type the personality of a horse. So money spent for professional training for a month or two or three (usually $100 to $150 per month) is a good investment, especially on two- and three-year-olds.

Nevertheless, some young horsemen want to train their own; so here are some basic principles, suggested by L. N. Sikes, a real Texas pro who has trained more than a thousand horses, including several world champions. (Although different trainers use slightly different techniques, you'll find that most of them follow the same basic principles.)

THE YOUNG COLT

Sikes likes to halter break the young colt when he is two or three weeks old. The colt is small enough at that age to catch and handle

34. Training a colt starts at two or three weeks of age, when he is easy to handle. L. N. Sikes backs the colt into a corner, with his mother nearby, holds him with knee under his belly and gently slips on halter.

without hurting you or him. Ease the colt up close to a fence or into a corner (Figure 34). Keep your knee and leg up under his belly so he can't kick and ease a soft rope halter on him.

After rubbing and petting the colt until he realizes that he isn't going to be hurt, Sikes starts teaching him to lead. He pulls the colt's head to the left until he moves his feet in that direction, then rewards him.

35. Teaching his colt to lead, James Davidson puts a nonslip loop over Dilly's hindquarters and leads her beside or behind her mother. After a day or two of this, the colt will lead alone.

Then he repeats the same thing to the right.

For straightaway leading, it's easiest to lead the colt beside his mother because he is eager to follow her. After a day or so of this, put a nonslip loop over the colt's hindquarters (Figure 35), run the rope through the halter and he will lead alone. "Do this ten minutes a day and in a week you'll have him leading well," promises Sikes.

61

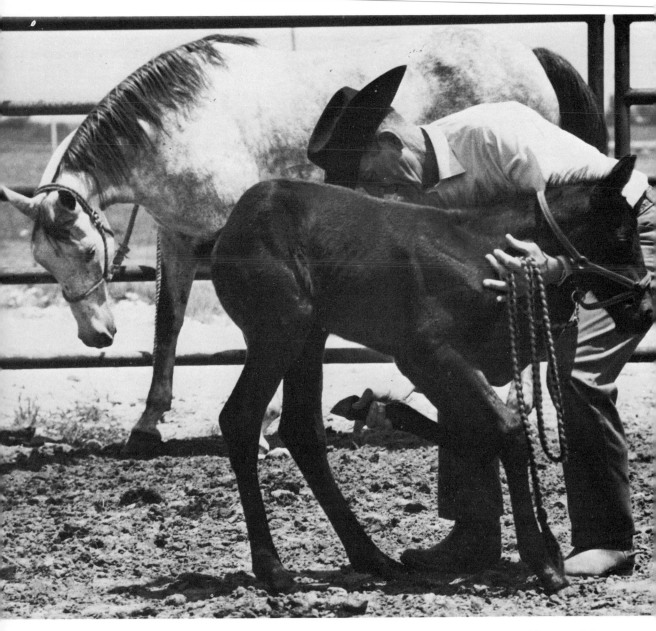

36. At an early age, get the colt accustomed to your hands. "Rub him, pet him and pick up his feet," advises L. N. Sikes, "so he will know you are a friend who is not going to hurt him."

During this kindergarten training, you also want the colt to get used to your hands (Figure 36). Rub him, pet him and pick up his feet until he recognizes you as a friend.

After a colt is halter broken, most trainers like to turn him out in the pasture with his mother "so he can learn to care for himself on his own." Because this is natural, colts seem to develop more self-confidence and desire to please than when raised around people from infancy.

Recently, I bought a beautiful two-year-old that had been in a stall or corral all his life. When I turned him to pasture, he must have thought, I'm free at last! because he started running, running, right through a barbed wire fence! So it was back to the stall for six weeks' treatment of cuts.

If colts can be raised in rough, rocky pastures, it's all the better; their feet will wear more evenly and they will become more surefooted.

Another good time to halter break a colt is at weaning, about six to eight months of age. "After two days away from his mother, a colt is lonesome and will take up with anybody or anything," says Sikes. "It's easy to make friends then. Call his name and talk to him. Within one hour, you can put a loop over his hindquarters and lead him."

37. Hobbling with a large soft rope around his front legs teaches the yearling to stand ground tied and not get excited if caught in wire. Some cowboys continue this; they hobble their old horse every time they dismount, rather than tie him to a fence.

38. L. N. Sikes eases saddle on, off and back several times, taking care not to excite the yearling.

THE YEARLING

The yearling colt is ready for first grade instruction. One of the first things Sikes teaches him is to "Whoa," always saying "Whoa" and calling his name. Then he hobbles (Figure 37) and sidelines the young horse (ties front foot to hind foot) so he will learn to stand still and won't get excited if caught in wire.

Also, he introduces the yearling to a saddle. First, he gently puts a saddle blanket on the young horse's back and moves it from head to tail until the colt is unafraid. After a day or two of this, he eases a saddle on, takes it off and puts it back on several times (Figure 38). Then he tightens the girth moderately and leads the colt around for ten or fifteen minutes. Following a few days of gentling like this, the yearling is again turned out to pasture.

39. Before riding a two-year-old, Sikes uses plowlines to drive, turn, stop and back up. The plowlines are run through the stirrups, which are tied together under the horse.

At about eighteen months of age, the young horse is ready for more training. Using plowlines (Figure 39), Sikes teaches him to drive, turn, and stop and back up. To make him supple (flex his neck freely) and to "set his head," he will tie the reins to the stirrups (Figure 40) or use rubber reins (Figure 41). This is merely a substitute for riding and a timesaver. Then the horse gets some light riding and introduction to leg pressures. (More on leg pressure and aids in Chapter 7.)

40. *To make a young horse supple and set his head, Sikes ties the bosal reins to the stirrups so that their weight pulls on his nose.*

"None of these lessons should last over thirty minutes," declares Sikes. "A colt at this age is unpredictable, and so don't try to teach him more than one thing at a time, and repeat it the same way day after day. Horses learn from repetition. Be gentle and patient but be firm—never let him forget that you are the boss."

"When a horse does what you want, reward him immediately by calling his name and petting him," continues Sikes. "If you correct him

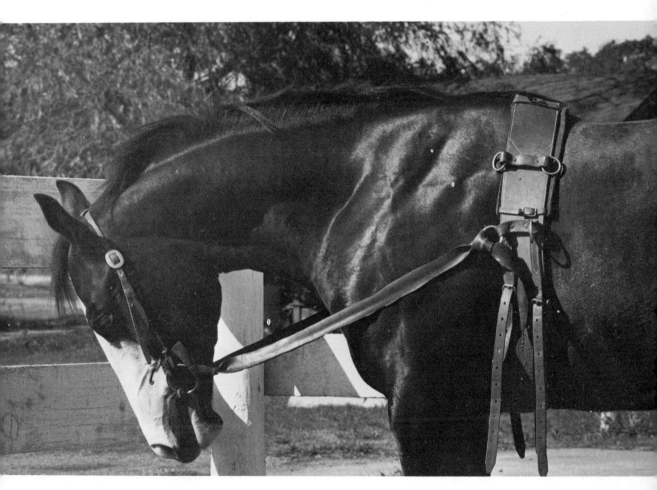

41. Another way to make a young horse supple and "give to the bit" is to use rubber reins, made from strips of old inner tube. There's no way the horse can hurt himself; after an hour or so, he'll go to a corner, tuck his head and stand.

with a switch or quirt, do it immediately and only once. Don't hit him twice more for revenge or you'll be worse off than when you started."

Some trainers use a quirt when training young horses. It's all right, if you use it sparingly and immediately *after* you give the horse the proper signal to move (leg pressure, reins or voice command). Never use the quirt *before* the signal.

Some trainers use spurs, too, but spurs are for the pros who know when and how to use them. If needed, spurs should be used to touch the horse, not to gouge him. More greenhorns have ruined horses with spurs—made them unresponsive—than have helped them.

During the first few months of riding, most trainers use a bosal so there is no danger of hurting the horse's mouth with bits. (See Chapter 6 for more on bits and bitting.)

THE TWO-YEAR-OLD

Now that your young horse is ready for riding, you will want to use aids that he understands. The four aids commonly used are your voice, hands, legs and weight. (More on aids in Chapter 7.)

After riding him a few days in a walk and trot, let him move into a lope or canter. And from the beginning, see that he lopes on the correct lead. On the left lead, the horse's left front and hind legs move out ahead of the right front and hind legs; on the right lead, it's just the opposite. When loping in a circle to the left, your horse should be on the left lead, front and rear; when loping in a circle to the right, he should be on the right lead. (More on leads in Chapter 5.)

Now is the time, also, to teach your horse to stop and to back up (Figure 42). Every time Sikes stops a young horse, he backs him up three or four steps and makes him stand there a few seconds. Then when ready to move from that spot, he pivots the horse on his hind feet (Figure 43). To pivot, he simply collects the horse (applies a little leg pressure

42. *When you stop a young horse, it's a good idea to back him a few steps. This teaches him to get his hind feet under him, which is essential for pivots and sharp turns.*

and takes up on the reins so that the horse gets his feet under him) and pulls the reins back slightly to one side. (More on pivots and stops in Chapter 5.) This gets the horse accustomed to stopping—without moving forward another two or three steps—and to turning on his rear feet.

43. When turning a young horse, teach him to turn on his hind feet. Pull him back until his hind feet are under him, then pull diagonally on the reins.

44. *In teaching your horse to back, start on the ground. Holding the reins near bosal or bit, push back in short jerks and command him to "Back, back." If necessary, nudge him on the shoulder or switch him on the forelegs at the same time.*

It usually takes an experienced horseman to put a good stop on a horse. If he is to "stick his tail in the ground," his back feet must be well under him. If he stops with his front feet, he'll bounce. "Some horses are born as good stoppers and others just can't do it," says Sikes. "But you can develop a better stop in most horses."

To teach your horse to back up, start on the ground. Hold the reins near the bosal or bit and push back in short jerks (Figure 44). At the same time, nudge him on the shoulder or switch him on the forelegs. After he has moved back two or three steps, stop and reward him. Repeat this, a little more each time over a period of a few days, until he knows what you want.

45. If your horse won't back, after you start riding him, ask a friend on the ground to switch him back while you repeatedly pull gently on the reins with both hands and release.

46. *Using a longe line, the author teaches a young horse basic maneuvers—gaits, leads, stop and rollback—before ever riding him. It's also a good way to exercise older horses.*

73

Next, you might get on the horse and ask a friend on the ground to switch him back while you pull gently on the reins (Figure 45). Keep your reins low so his head won't fly up. And apply the pressure (on his nose or mouth) in short light jerks so his mouth won't gape open. In other words, apply the pressure lightly and release, apply pressure and release.

Now when your horse knows what it is to back up, you should do it this way: Collect him by applying leg pressure and take up on the reins (he can't back until his feet are under him); put weight in your stirrups (he must hump his back slightly so this takes some pressure off his back); pull lightly on the reins.

Some horsemen train their young horses on a longe line, which is a rope about fifteen to twenty feet long that permits the horse to travel in a circle around you (Figure 46). Longeing also is a good way to exercise an older horse without having to saddle and ride him.

At the Spanish Riding School of Vienna, home of the famed Lippizaner stallions, instructors teach horses (and students) most of the basic maneuvers—gaits, leads, stops, rollbacks, etc.—on the longe. In fact, they work young horses (starting at age four) for one year on the ground before riding them, using the longe, the short rein and the long rein.

Most trainers in this country like the longe, too, except for roping horses. "We want a roping horse, when on the end of a rope, to run straight back, rather than around us," explains Sikes, who also is a professional roper.

Here's something to remember about training: Every time you get on or move around your horse, you are training him. You are forming habits in his mind—good or bad—so think about everything you do and try to make them good habits.

5.
Gaits, Leads and Stops

Every rider expects his horse to perform well in various gaits. Yet how many riders can accurately describe the different gaits? If you want to be an informed horseman, and maybe surprise your friends, learn the sequence of hoofbeats in the basic gaits.

The three natural gaits are the walk, trot and canter (also called lope or gallop, which actually is faster than the canter).

The *walk* is a slow, flat-footed four-beat gait (Figure 47). The sequence of hoofbeats is (1) right front, (2) left hind, (3) left front and (4) right hind. In the walk, a horse never has less than two or more than three feet on the ground at one time; thus he has a triangular base of support. A good stride is desirable, which means the rear hoofprints will contact or overreach the front hoofprints.

The *trot* is a rapid two-beat diagonal gait, which means that the right front foot and left hind foot move together (Figure 48). As a pair of diagonals, they take off and strike the ground at the same time. Likewise, the left front foot and right hind foot move together. As the horse moves from one pair of diagonals to the other pair, all four feet are off the ground for an instant.

A *jog trot* is a slow smooth gait used in Western Pleasure classes. In an *extended trot*, the horse lengthens his stride and thus covers more ground.

The *canter* is an easy three-beat gait with rhythm (Figure 49). The front foot that moves out farther ahead is called the lead foot; and the hind foot on the same side moves out ahead of the other hind foot. A

47. In the walk, a four-beat gait, note that only one foot is off the ground. The sequence of hoofbeats is (1) right front, (2) left hind, (3) left front and (4) right hind.

48. In the trot, a two-beat diagonal gait, right front and left rear feet move together and left front and right rear feet (both on the ground here) move together.

horse can lead on either his right or left feet and should be able to do
both with equal ease. When circling to the left, he should always be on
the left lead; to the right, on the right lead.

The sequence of hoofbeats, when on the left lead, is (1) right hind,
(2) the diagonal left hind and right front feet together and (3) left front.
On the right lead, it's (1) left hind, (2) the diagonal right hind and left
front and (3) right front.

49. In the canter or lope, a three-beat gait with rhythm, the horse may be on right lead or left lead. Here, he is on right lead and sequence of hoofbeats is (1) left hind, (2) right hind and left front together and (3) right front.

Other gaits are: the *running walk,* a smooth diagonal four-beat gait, where the hind foot oversteps the diagonal front foot; the *pace,* a fast two-beat gait, with the front and hind feet on the same side moving together; the *fox trot,* a nodding trot, where the hind foot strikes ground an instant before the diagonal front foot; and the *rack* or *single-foot,* a fast, evenly timed, high-stepping four-beat gait, where the sequence of hoofbeats is (1) right hind, (2) right front, (3) left hind and (4) left front.

78

CORRECT LEADS

In Western riding or reining, your horse must go on the correct lead, either right or left, when you request it. Beginning riders usually have to look down and see the horse's feet to tell which lead he is on (the lead front foot goes out farther ahead, as in Figure 49, and is the last to strike the ground). But with a little practice and concentration, you can tell by merely glancing down at your horse's shoulders. And with more practice, you can feel which lead he is on. (Your body tends to twist with the lead, and your foot will move ahead with the horse's lead foot.)

Now, how do you get your horse on the correct lead? There are several ways; and if you have a way that is working well, don't change. But I like the method used by Darrell Davidson, a trainer and riding instructor in Texas. He first teaches his young horses to respond to leg pressure—to move forward when both legs are pressed, to the side when one leg is pressed (Figure 50).

When starting from a stop, he (1) collects the horse, (2) uses his opposite leg (off-lead side) for pressure just behind the girth, (3) leans forward a little from the hips up, and (4) pulls the reins diagonally across the withers *in the opposite direction* from the desired lead.

"You can feel him raise up to take the correct lead," says Davidson. "The diagonal reining (not neck reining) and the opposite leg pressure will make him twist and step off on the correct hind lead (Figure 51). And if he takes the proper hind lead, he always will take the proper front lead."

Some trainers start a young horse by trotting in a small circle and applying outside leg pressure until he takes the correct lead. Then they keep making the circle larger until it's as big as the arena. Therefore, the horse relates the correct lead to the leg pressure.

Beginners, particularly those with short legs, often use the fence and

50. *Your horse must respond to leg pressure—move forward with pressure from both legs, to the side with pressure from one leg. Here, Darrell Davidson side passes to his right by pressing with his left leg behind the girth and canting horse's head to the left.*

51. *To put horse in the left lead, pull the reins diagonally to the right and press with your right leg until the horse twists and steps off on the left hind lead. If a horse takes correct hind lead, he always will take the correct front lead.*

52. *A little rider on a big horse may have to use a fence to get the correct lead. For left lead, (1) pull your horse toward right fence, (2) shift weight slightly to left stirrup, (3) neck rein to the left and (4) nudge him with your right heel.*

a shift of weight. For example, if they want the left lead, they (1) pull the horse to the right fence, (2) shift weight slightly to the left stirrup (but don't lean), (3) neck rein him to the left and (4) nudge him with the right heel (Figure 52).

53. Cross-leading. Note that horse is leading with his left front foot and right hind foot, causing him to be disunited.

Top trainers don't recommend this method, because you should be able to put your horse on the correct lead anywhere, any time, without a fence. "If the horse is well trained, he should go on lead without the judge seeing the rider do anything," declares Davidson.

83

Some old nags are one-leaded, usually because an inexperienced rider has let them travel in one lead always. If your horse only wants to go in the left lead, for example, Davidson suggests trotting in a small circle to the right. Go faster and faster until he takes the right lead. Then continue riding in small circles for several days or until he feels just as comfortable to the right as to the left.

Another frequent problem is that a horse gets on the correct front lead but "drops" his hind lead, called *cross-leading* or being "disunited" (Figure 53). Unless caught early, this is difficult to correct. One way that sometimes works is to reach over with a long switch or twisted baling wire and hit him on the dragging hind lead. This usually causes him to draw up that foot to the correct position.

CHANGING LEADS

With practice, your horse can make a flying change of leads with speed, smoothness and efficiency. Expertly trained horses can do it straightaway, but most Western Pleasure horses are trained to do it in the Figure 8.

You and your horse can do it well, if you will remember three things: (1) use the proper aids, (2) cue him at the proper time and (3) do it slowly at first.

Trainer Davidson lopes a young horse in a small circle, say to the right, then drops to a trot for three or four steps before pushing him into the opposite lead. The next day, he slows him to a trot for only two steps, and the following day one step.

"After six or eight days of this, you can pull up (but don't let him stop), and he'll change himself," says Davidson. "The aids are (1) push with your leg the way you want him to go, (2) pick up on the reins a little and (3) touch him on the neck (with reins) the way you want him to go."

Some trainers shift their weight at the same time, which is okay if you don't lean way over. You can shift your weight in the stirrups without leaning; *but stay on top of your horse!*

The time to cue him with your leg is when his back feet are on the ground or his lead foot is in the air. This alerts him; then you rein him when the lead foot hits the ground. "This may seem awkward the first few times, but you'll soon get the feel of it and do it smoothly," concludes Davidson. "It isn't necessary to gouge your horse and speed up when changing leads, as so many young riders do."

PUTTING A STOP ON YOUR HORSE

Whatever you plan to do with your horse—pleasure riding, reining, roping or cutting—he'll do it better if he can "stick his tail in the ground and die" (Figure 54). Not every horse can do this; some just aren't built for quick stops. But you can help him, and you can develop an acceptable stop on most horses.

"Whatever you do, don't bust out wide open and haul back on the reins," advises trainer Davidson. "Get him to stopping first at the walk, then the trot, at a short lope after several days and finally when wide open. To do it right may take months."

The aids that Davidson uses are (1) squeeze with your legs, (2) say "Ho," (3) sit back deep in the saddle (you should have been leaning forward with most of your weight in the stirrups) and (4) pull up on the reins. "The leg pressure is to alert the horse," he says, "and throwing your weight back, when properly timed, drives his hind feet up under him. Pull on the reins no harder than you have to; then release the pressure so the horse can use his head to maintain his balance."

Now, what is the proper timing? Squeeze when the lead foot is off the ground and the hind feet are getting ready to come off. As his hind

54. A good stop takes months to develop. Rider Jan Montreuil keeps reining hand low, horse's head low and his front feet near the ground. Most judges prefer a stop with three or four feet on ground, rather than the spectacular two-hind-leg stop.

feet come up, shift your weight back and start making contact with his mouth. But don't jerk. Jerking is what hurts a horse's mouth, makes his head fly up and mouth gape open.

Another thing on timing: If you "apply the brakes" when the horse is stretched out and his front feet are in the air, you force him to throw all his weight on his front feet and he'll bounce.

A good stop is on three or four feet. If on three, the fore foot is up slightly, ready to turn or roll back either way. Some amateur riders try for spectacular sliding stops, with both front feet up in the air. But most good horsemen don't like this, because the horse is not balanced and can fall over backward. The really good stop is performed with rhythm and balance, easily and smoothly.

55. *In teaching a horse to pivot, Darrell Davidson walks him in a small circle, getting smaller and smaller, until the horse has hind feet planted and walks around them on front feet. Here, he holds hind end with right heel, pulls reins diagonally to left.*

56. *Next, in teaching horse to pivot, ride about three feet from a high fence, stop, collect horse and gently pull the reins in the direction of the fence. Fence causes horse to get back on hind feet and pivot 180 degrees.*

PIVOTS AND ROLLBACKS

Again, work on these slow and easy. To start a new horse, trainer Davidson walks him in a small circle, getting smaller and smaller until the horse's hind feet are still. Then he pulls the reins back diagonally across the withers and the horse walks around with his front feet, like the spokes of a wagon wheel, while his hind feet stay still, like the hub (Figure 55). He does this three or four times a day, both to the right and left, for several days.

Then Davidson moves to a high fence. While walking about three feet from the fence, he stops, collects the horse and gently pulls diagonally in the direction of the fence (Figure 56). The fence forces the horse to get back on his hind feet and pivot 180 degrees. If the horse doesn't want to hold his hind feet in place, Davidson uses a broom handle against the hind leg, which "will really hold 'em."

Later, he slowly pivots the horse 360 degrees, so he doesn't get the habit of jumping back and forth, and finally speeds it up. "Pivots are easy to put on a horse," he concludes, "but he has got to be on his hind legs or it is a physical impossibility to pivot smoothly. All he can do is hop and rear."

Rollbacks are a little tougher, and rightly so, because you have taught your horse to "stop and die" and now you want him to stop and do something. (A rollback is a turnaround in place, in which the horse pivots on his rear feet to reverse his direction. It's much like the military drill, "To the rear, march.")

Starting with the walk and trot, Davidson stops and pivots in both directions. Then he goes into a short lope, stops, pivots and kicks out into a short lope. Finally, he crowds the horse and speeds up the complete rollback (Figure 57 and 58).

After the horse is trained, you can do it this way: (1) stop, (2) give the horse some rein so he can regain his balance, (3) pull the rein diagonally for a 180-degree pivot and (4) push off into a lope.

If done right, the rollback is coordinated, smooth and easy for you to stay on the horse. If uncoordinated, it's rough and hard to stay on.

All these things—correct leads, change of leads, stops, pivots and rollbacks—are exhibited in reining patterns and in cutting. Remember

89

57. *Beginning of the rollback, which is a fast change of direction. You stop the horse and, while the hind feet are still under him, pull diagonally on the reins to start the 180-degree pivot.*

58. *Completion of the rollback. With the hind feet almost in place, the horse rolls back over his hocks and pushes off into a lope. Rider may use only one hand for reining.*

that the best trained horse is the one that does them smoothly and efficiently, without any noticeable cues from the rider or with the least obvious cues.

Another thing to remember about reining patterns: they vary at different shows, and good reining horses sometimes lose out because the rider doesn't know the pattern. This can be very embarrassing. Most judges call for AQHA Reining Pattern No. 1 (Figure 116 in Chapter 9), but when the competition is stiff they sometimes call for No. 3 or No. 4. So before you enter a reining contest, make sure you know all four AQHA reining patterns, described in the AQHA Official Handbook.

6.
Bits, Saddles
and Equipment

If your horse is being pinched, rubbed or hurt in any way, he won't perform to the best of his ability. Many young horsemen don't realize that differently shaped horses require different shapes or types of equipment. But they do. So you should select bits, saddle and other equipment just as if you were selecting a pair of boots for yourself—make sure they fit.

BITS AND BITTING

"No mouth, no horse," is an old expression of horsemen. This is the steering system on your horse and, like an auto, a horse isn't a pleasure to ride unless the steering system functions smoothly and efficiently.

"I have seen more horses ruined by improper bitting or improper use of bits than by anything else," declares Buster Parish, who has trained horses for twenty years and now operates the Salt Grass Saddlery in Houston where he comes in daily contact with many horsemen. So that you won't unintentionally hurt or ruin your horse this way, you must understand the horse's mouth and how the bit works.

The mouthpiece of the bit rests on the bars of the horse's mouth, which is the portion of the gums between his front teeth (incisors) and back teeth (premolars and molars). The bars are covered with very thin and sensitive skin. If you keep pressure on the bars constantly or injure them with excessively hard pulls, the nerves become numb and insensi-

59. *The bosal, a braided rawhide noseband that applies pressure to nose and chin when reins are pulled, is good for starting a young horse. It is not recommended for precision reining, but there's no danger of hurting his mouth.*

94

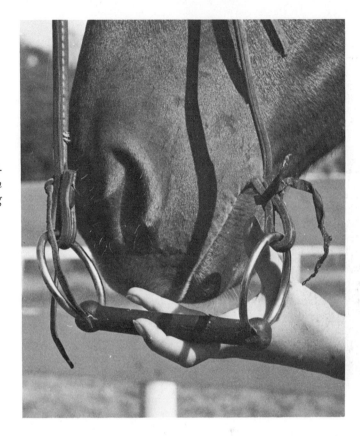

60. His first bit. A rubber snaffle, flexible and covered with rubber, can't hurt the young horse's mouth.

tive. Then the bars become tough and the horse is said to have a "tough mouth" or a "cold mouth."

For horses that are ready to ride but have had no training with bits, Parish recommends the bosal (Figure 59). This is a braided rawhide noseband that applies pressure, when reins are pulled, to the sensitive part of the nose and to the chin. Using the bosal for a few weeks or a few months, Parish gets the horse to stopping, turning and backing; then he switches to a snaffle bit.

For yearlings, which he can familiarize with bits before it is time to start riding them, Parish starts with the rubber snaffle, which has a flexible mouthpiece covered with rubber (Figure 60). He teaches them

95

61. With rubber snaffle bit and plowlines through bitting harness, Buster Parish teaches the yearling to drive, stop, turn and back up. Driving also makes him supple—teaches him to tuck nose and flex at the poll—which makes him easier to rein later.

to drive, using a driving harness (Figure 61) or plowlines run through the stirrups.

If the young horse tends to throw his head or carry it high (he should flex at the poll, tuck his chin and keep his head low when the reins are pulled) Parish attaches the rubber bit to the reining harness with strips of an old auto inner tube (Figure 41 in Chapter 4). "There's no way a colt can hurt himself with this hookup," he says, "so I leave it on him (in a stall or small pen) an hour or two at a time, for several days in a row. When the colt goes to a corner, tucks his head to relieve the pressure and acts comfortable, he has learned his lesson."

62. *Draw reins, attached to girth and run through ring of snaffle bit, keep horse from stargazing. Sheri Finley found that they made her horse supple, helped her become Championship Horseman at Texas 4-H Horse Show.*

Some trainers accomplish the same thing by tieing the reins to the stirrups (Figure 40 in Chapter 4). The stirrups are pulled forward just enough to apply a little pressure; but when the colt tucks his chin, the stirrups hang straight and relieve the pressure.

Next, Parish switches to the metal ring snaffle or mule bit. It is flexible, and the pull of the reins is direct so you aren't likely to hurt the horse's mouth. If the horse still tends to stargaze when you ride him, use draw reins (Figure 62). You must teach him *early* to carry that head low and to flex at the poll or he'll probably be hard to handle for the

63. A good training device for the young horse or an older horse that carries his head too high is the running martingale. It attaches to the girth and has rings through which the reins thread.

rest of his life. The running martingale (Figure 63) will accomplish the same thing as draw reins.

After the horse becomes accustomed to a bit in his mouth and responds reasonably well, Parish moves on to the shank snaffle (Figure 64). With a curb strap or curb chain, the shank acts as a lever to increase the pressure on the bars and give you more control. If you have a light hand and your horse is responding well, this bit may suit you from now on.

If you feel the need for a stronger bit, however, Parish recommends the grazing bit with a low or medium port (Figure 65). These bits come with high ports, too, which usually are needed only if the horse flips his

64. *The shank snaffle bit has a flexible mouthpiece, which makes it easier on the horse. Yet it has a curb chain and shanks so that you have plenty of control. It is good for any horse, if his mouth hasn't been damaged.*

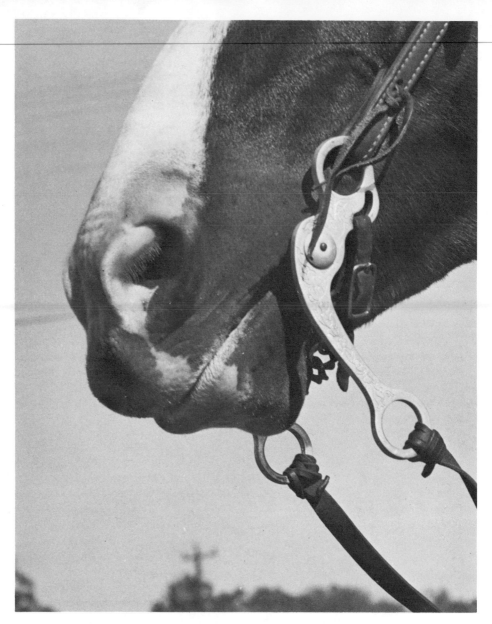

65. The grazing bit with a medium port is the most common kind. It has a curb chain and shanks six to nine inches long so you have plenty of control. The longer the shank the more severe it is. Shanks curve backward so horse can graze.

tongue over the low port. The shanks or cheeks vary from six to nine inches in length, the longer ones giving more leverage. The "grazing bit" means that the shanks turn back at an angle so that the horse can graze with the bit in his mouth.

"Grazing bits can be very severe on a horse's mouth, particularly if you're hardhanded," concludes Parish. "They should be used with instant pressure *and instant release,* as soon as the horse responds correctly. Never rear back on the reins and hold the pressure. This will kill the nerves in the bars and give your horse a tough mouth."

The curb strap or curb chain (it should be a smooth, flat chain) should be adjusted so it applies no pressure when the reins are loose. But it should tighten up as soon as you pick up on the reins. As a rule of thumb, when the curb is loose, you should be able to slip two fingers under it (Figure 66).

66. *A curb strap should be adjusted so it applies no pressure when reins are loose but tightens up as soon as you pick up on reins. It's properly adjusted, when loose, if you can slip two fingers under it.*

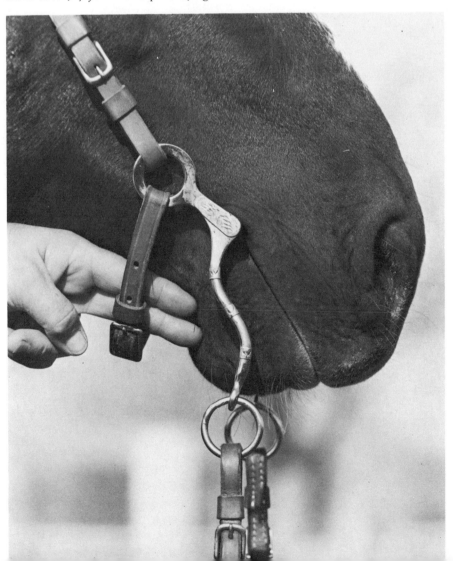

67. *The mechanical hackamore has no mouthpiece but is hinged to apply pressure on nose and under jaw. It's often used by barrel racers and ropers; good for quick stops but not good for precision reining.*

The mechanical hackamore (Figure 67), which does not have a mouthpiece, frequently is used in place of a bit. It hinges so that pressure is applied to the hard bones of the nose and the under jaw. But the mechanical hackamore doesn't give instant and precise control, like a bit; and for this reason, most professional horsemen don't use it for reining or pleasure. It is widely used, however, for barrel racing and roping, where fast starts and sudden stops are required.

SADDLES

Everybody takes pride in owning a good-looking saddle. But more important, does it fit you and the horse? For a good performance, it must be comfortable for both.

68. The parts of a Western saddle.

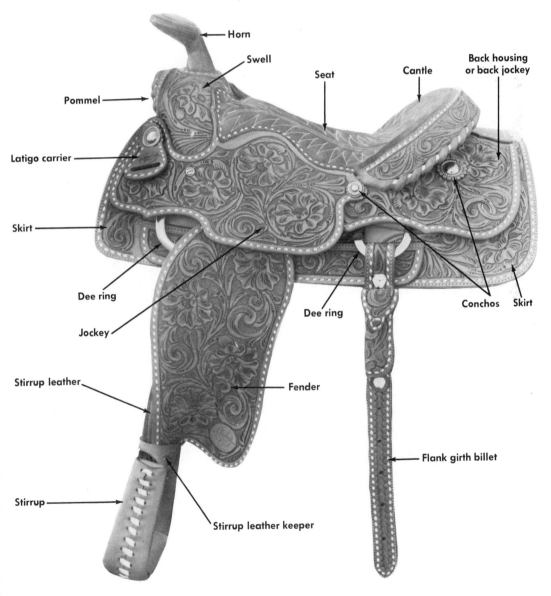

Trees or frames for Western saddles come in three basic types: (1) the full Quarter Horse tree, which fits most Quarter-type horses, (2) the semi-Quarter Horse tree, for horses with higher withers, and (3) the Arabian tree, which is flatter and has shorter bars. Most good trees are made of wood and covered with rawhide. But some of the new ones are plastic. (For parts of a saddle, see Figure 68.)

69. A built-up padded seat is comfortable to ride. But it holds you back against the cantle, making it difficult to shift your weight forward as desired in horsemanship or equitation classes.

70. *A good all-around saddle. This one has a relatively flat quilted seat, a thirteen-inch swell, and a fifteen-inch seat. Similar saddles cost $200 to $500, depending on quality and trim.*

The seats are usually fifteen inches long, from cantle to fork, but longer seats for large people and shorter seats for children are available. Most new saddles have padded or quilted seats, some of which are built up in front to hold you back against the cantle (Figure 69). These built-up seats are comfortable but they make it almost impossible to

71. *If properly cared for, a good saddle will outlast several horses. Mary Ann Ball has her saddle on a good type of saddle rack. Stirrups are twisted and a broom handle run through them; leathers are dampened so they will hang straight when on horse.*

shift your weight forward, as desired in performance classes (Figure 86, Chapter 7).

The swells come in three general types, too: (1) roping, which is narrow, making it easy for the rider to get off the horse; (2) cutting, which is wider and helps hold your thighs in the saddle; and (3) general purpose, which is best for most uses (Figure 70).

There are many other differences in saddles, so if you aren't familiar with them be sure to consult a horseman or good saddlemaker before buying. I've seen too many disappointed kids stuck with a misfit saddle, given to them by parents who know nothing about horses. And a saddle, if properly cared for, usually outlasts several horses (Figure 71).

OTHER EQUIPMENT

If your saddle doesn't fit your horse perfectly, you should use two blankets or a blanket and pad. (Most trainers use a pad under a blanket all the time anyhow.) The better blankets are made of wool and the best pads of hair, because they absorb more moisture and are less likely to rub the horse.

Every horse owner needs one or two halters. Your everyday halter, of rope or heavy leather, should be strong enough so it won't break if your horse is tied and becomes scared (and the gentlest horse occasionally gets scared). Caution: When tieing your horse, do it with a halter—bridles aren't made for tieing.

Another caution: Don't leave a halter on your horse in the pasture, as I see a lot of kids doing. True, he may be easier to catch, but he might get the halter caught on some object and wouldn't be able to get loose.

You'll need a strong lead rope, too, about six to eight feet long. If it has a snap, make sure the snap is strong enough to hold a scared horse.

107

72. *Barrel racers, like 4-H'er Helen Malone, use a breast harness to keep the saddle from sliding back and a tiedown to keep the horse's head from going excessively high on fast turns.*

(See how to tie a horse, Figure 26, in Chapter 3.)

Bridles come in many styles and designs. The kind of headstall to use is strictly a matter of personal preference—some have browbands and throatlatches, others have shaped or split earpieces.

Reins vary greatly, too. Many kids prefer narrow leather reins ($\frac{3}{8}$ inch to $\frac{1}{2}$ inch wide), but I find that wider reins (about $\frac{3}{4}$ inch) give me a better grip and better control of the horse.

Most Western riders these days like breast straps (also called breast collars or roping harness), although they are not necessary for casual riding. Of course, ropers and barrel racers need them to help keep the saddle in place (Figure 72). I agree that they look nice, however, and usually use one myself.

A nosepiece or tiedown (Figure 72) is another piece of equipment that most young riders want at one time or another. If you are roping or barrel racing or if your horse carries his head excessively high, a tiedown will hold his head down. Otherwise, I see no need for it.

Skid boots for your horse's hind feet will protect his fetlocks, if you are roping or making sliding stops while reining. Without them, if your horse really sits down on hard ground, he'll burn his fetlocks and become afraid to make a sliding stop.

There are many other items of equipment, which are nice to have if you need them for a specific purpose. But in general, you'll be better off to keep your equipment simple and in good condition.

A good horseman cleans his leather equipment after each use. Glycerine saddle soap is best. The Royal Canadian Mounted Police often put on two or three performances a day, and they saddle soap their equipment two or three times a day! Also, leather will stay flexible, be safe and last much longer if you treat it occasionally with Lexol or neat's-foot oil. Leather equipment should be stored in a dry place. And if it does get wet, dry it at normal room temperature—never dry leather with heat.

7.
Western Horsemanship

"The country is full of good riders, but good horsemen are scarce," says Blair Smith of California, who is a judge for the American Horse Show Association (AHSA) and the American Quarter Horse Association (AQHA). "Many young riders like to ride like Indians and cowboys on TV, which may be fun for beginners, but they are not good horsemen."

Whether you plan to enter a show or want to ride just for pleasure, safely, you should *learn and practice* good horsemanship. If you don't practice it every time you ride, you'll slip up sometime in the show ring and never know it. One of my good 4-H Horse Club members bombed out at a recent District 4-H Horse Show, for example, when he backed his horse with both hands on the reins. "Of course, I know better, Mr. Ball," he told me after the class. "But Amy is just learning to back and I've been practicing that way."

In the show classes, there's a difference between Western Pleasure and Western Horsemanship (sometimes called Western Equitation). In Pleasure, the horse is being judged; in Horsemanship, the rider is judged. But in either case, you and your horse will make a better showing if you are a good horseman.

What do judges look for in Western Horsemanship? I have asked many of them, and each gives a slightly different answer. It varies by parts of the country, too, especially from the West Coast to the Southwest. But nearly all judges and instructors agree on the basic principles out-

73. *A winning horsewoman, like nineteen-year-old Susan DiBiase, knows the importance of a neat appearance. In Western Horsemanship, you must wear a western hat and boots; chaps, spurs and other attire are optional.*

lined in this chapter. If you follow these, you'll show well. Even if you don't plan to show, you'll still enjoy your horse more.

Proper Attire and Equipment

A neat appearance by the rider and horse is important, but gaudy dress is undesirable. You must wear a Western hat and boots; spurs are optional. Jeans or Western pants are preferable; other attire is optional (Figure 73).

Any type of stock saddle may be used; a breast collar is optional. Either a snaffle, curb or grazing bit may be used, with a curb strap or chain at least one half-inch wide. The reins must be of leather and split (Figure 77), unless a romal (Figure 81) is used. In some classes, a hackamore with split leather or split rope reins may be used. No mechanical hackamores or tiedowns are permitted in Western Pleasure.

Mounting and Dismounting

Seldom will you be asked to dismount in Western Pleasure and not always in Western Horsemanship. But if you don't know how to mount a horse properly, can you call yourself a horseman?

There are several ways you can mount, but I know only two that are safe, comfortable and pleasing to judges. The first way (Figures 74 to 77), which you'll see more often in the Southwest and Midwest, is to: (1) Stand even with the saddle facing your horse. (2) Take up your reins evenly and hold them in your left hand. (3) Place your left hand firmly on the horse's neck, just in front of his withers, and your right hand on the saddle horn. (4) Raise your left foot into the stirrup and brace your knee against the horse (Figure 74). (If you need to steady the stirrup

74. *The proper way to mount: Stand facing your horse, gather reins evenly in your left hand and place your right hand on saddle horn, raise your left foot into stirrup and brace your knee against the horse.*

for your foot, do it with your right hand before reaching for the horn.) (5) With a spring, push straight up with your right foot until you are standing in the left stirrup, leaning forward just enough to maintain your balance (Figure 75). (6) Swing your right leg over the saddle (Figure 76) and be seated (Figure 77).

Try mounting first by the numbered steps; then do it all in one continuous and graceful motion.

75. *Then, with a spring, push straight up with your right foot until you are stand-ing in the left stirrup, leaning forward just enough to maintain your balance. Left hand can rest on the horse's neck.*

76. *Swing your right leg over the saddle and be seated. Horse should not move during mounting; hold him with reins in your left hand, if necessary.*

77. *When seated, you should be sitting erect in the saddle, your feet deep in the stirrups and heels down. Your left hand should hold reins just above saddle horn, while right hand rests on thigh.*

To dismount, it's almost the reverse: (1) Put your left hand (holding reins) on the horse's neck. (2) Place your right hand on the saddle horn, lean slightly forward and shift your weight to the left stirrup. (3) Swing your right leg over the saddle and step straight down. (4) As soon as your right foot hits the ground, lower your left heel so it slips out of the stirrup and lower it to the ground. (5) Leaving the right rein over the horse's neck, keep the left rein in your left hand and face the horse's head.

The other approved way to mount (Figures 78 to 81) is to: (1) Stand by your horse's shoulder, facing the rear, with romal or reins in your left hand on the horse's neck. (2) with your right hand, twist the stirrup 180 degrees and insert your left foot (Figure 78). (3) Then put your right hand on the saddle horn and brace your left knee against the horse (Figure 79). (4) Next, swing your right leg over the saddle (Figure 80) and be seated. (5) Now move the romal from the left to the right and hold it in your right hand against your right thigh (Figure 81).

To dismount, first move the romal to your left side, across the saddle horn, and reverse the above procedure.

78. Another approved way to mount, sometimes preferred in the Far West: Stand by your horse's shoulder, facing the rear and holding romal or reins in your left hand on the horse's neck. With your right hand, twist the stirrup 180 degrees and insert your left foot.

79. *Then put your right hand on the saddle horn and brace your left knee against the horse.*

80. Next, with a spring, push up with your right foot until standing in your stirrup, swing your right leg over the saddle and be seated.

81. *When seated, you should be sitting erect with weight on the balls of your feet and your heels down. With a romal, your left hand should be directly over the saddle horn while your right hand holds the loose end against your right thigh. Note that romal is held by all four fingers, with bit end down.*

THE WESTERN SEAT

Ride tall in the saddle! This means you should keep your head up, your body erect and your heels low. At the same time, you should ride relaxed so you look comfortable. But don't go to sleep or you'll get *behind* your horse. You must be *with* your horse but thinking *ahead* of him. So look relaxed but be alert and ready.

Let's analyze the Western seat, first when you're sitting still (Figure 77). Your stirrups should be short enough so that when you stand up your crotch will clear the saddle by three or four inches—room for four fingers. Then when you sit down, your knees will be bent slightly and in a good position to serve as shock absorbers. Your kneecap should line up vertically with the swell of your saddle and the toe of your boot. Thus, when you press down with your feet (heels down, don't tiptoe), you will rise up rather than push back in the saddle.

Your feet should be well into the stirrups so your weight is on the balls or arch of your feet (Figure 82). Even when sitting still, you should have a little of your weight (about 5 to 10 percent) in the stirrups. This gives you balance and security, in case the horse jumps suddenly. Keep your heels down, toes pointed ahead or slightly outward.

Hold your reins in your left hand, with the loose ends hanging on the left side of your horse. (If you are using the romal, popular in California, it would be held in your right hand on the right side of the horse—see Figure 81.) In most classes, the reins may be held with your index finger between them (Figure 83), which gives slightly more control than with no finger between them. Place your right hand on your right thigh.

Your horse should work on a loose rein but not so loose that it is sloppy or flapping. A good rule of thumb is to have a tight rein (contact with the horse's mouth) when your hand is directly over the saddle horn.

82. *In the Cow Country, old cowboys ride with their feet "deep in the stirrups," with weight on the arch of foot, as shown. Some show judges, however, prefer the heel back slightly, so weight is on the ball of foot. In either case, keep your heels down.*

83. Index finger between the reins is permitted in most classes. It allows you to make slight adjustments in rein length and thus gives you better control. With romal, this is not permitted in shows.

Then, by moving your hand forward slightly, you have a loose rein. If you have to take up on your horse for a quick stop, you still have room to do it without hitting yourself in the stomach or without raising your hand too high.

84. To move out at a walk, lean slightly foward from your hips up, put a little weight in your stirrups and cue your horse with leg pressure. Ride on your crotch.

Now, to move out in a walk (Figure 84), you lean slightly forward, from the hips up, put a little more weight in the stirrups (about 10 to 20 percent), and cue your horse with leg pressure. Your thighs and upper calves should always be in contact with the horse. This helps him know what you want and helps you maintain your balance. You should ride on your crotch, not with your seat back on the cantle.

125

85. *To trot, lean a bit more forward, put a little more weight in your stirrups and apply more leg pressure. Weight in the stirrups will help keep you from bouncing, because your knees and ankles act as shock absorbers when your heels are down.*

To trot (Figure 85), you lean a bit more forward, put a little more weight in the stirrups (about 20 to 30 percent) and apply more leg pressure. This weight in the stirrups will help keep you from bouncing, because with your legs bent slightly and your heels down, your knees and ankles act as shock absorbers.

To lope (Figure 86), you lean still farther forward from the hips up (but don't stoop), put more weight in the stirrups (40 to 60 percent) and

86. *To lope, lean still farther forward (don't stoop), put more weight in your stirrups and cue your horse for the correct lead. Reins should be reasonably loose but not flopping.*

cue him for the correct lead as described in Chapter 5. Some judges, especially in the Far West, prefer that you stay erect at all times. But I find it more natural, and acceptable by most judges, to lean slightly forward when loping.

In all gaits, keep your elbows near your body so they don't "flap and wave." Your right hand should be carried in a comfortable position; in a walk, on your right thigh is a good place for it. When trotting or loping, however, it might be more natural for you to bend the right elbow and carry your hand near your belt. Or you can leave your hand on your right thigh; it's optional. The idea is to stay poised and balanced, so that you move gracefully and in rhythm with your horse.

When the judge asks you to reverse directions, turn to the inside of the ring, away from the fence. Before turning, however, it's good manners and good showmanship to look around for other riders; otherwise, you might cause a traffic jam. My son Chuck surely endorses this—now. At the State 4-H Horse Show, he and another contestant were vying for first place in Western Pleasure; the judges had narrowed it down to two. But when they called for "reverse at a lope," Chuck turned into the other horse, causing his horse to break gait, and that ended it. Chuck placed second.

A member of our 4-H Club, eighteen-year-old Cindy Lea, reminds me that two other things are necessary to win blue ribbons—concentration and dedication. Cindy should know, for with Bay Bandit Josie, which is the only horse she owns and which she trained herself, she has won twenty-five blue ribbons in the last two years. The climax—for her, me and the thirty-five members of our club—was at the State Fair of Texas when, competing against professionals from all over the country, she was Grand Champion in Western Pleasure!

Some Don'ts

In conclusion, here are some DON'Ts based on the mistakes or errors that judges say they see most often:

DON'T go in the arena with an ungroomed horse or with dirty equipment; look as though you came to win.

DON'T use excessively loose or flopping reins; be able to stop your horse without hitting yourself in the stomach.

DON'T tiptoe in the stirrups when trotting or loping; adjust your stirrups and keep your heels low.

DON'T slump in the saddle; keep your body erect and balanced and look proud and happy.

DON'T use "body English" or lean to the side when cueing your horse; stay on top.

DON'T flap your elbows; keep them near your body and your free hand on your thigh or near your belt.

DON'T push your feet forward and your seat back on the cantle; ride on your thighs and crotch.

DON'T kick your horse or gouge him with spurs; train him to move out with leg pressures.

DON'T use two hands or change hands on the reins during a class; also, don't touch the saddle horn or cantle with your free hand, unless your horse spooks.

DON'T turn toward the rail or pass another rider on the rail side; pass and turn to the inside.

DON'T rear back and pull high on the reins to stop; cue at the right time and keep your hands low.

DON'T "go to sleep" or gaze at the audience; keep alert and watch the judge out of the corner of your eye.

8.
How to Show a Winner

If you're proud of your "broomtail"—be it a $200 nag or a $2,000 registered animal—you'll probably want to show him occasionally. That's where the fun is, where the challenge is! (See Figure 87.)

87. Show day—that's what appeals to most young horsemen, whether they own a $200 nag or a $2,000 registered animal. In most states, there is a show within fifty miles of every horse owner nearly every summer weekend.

In our 4-H Club shows, every member shows his or her horse at halter and enters performance events of his or her choice. Usually, a horse performs well either in rail events, like Western Pleasure, Western Horsemanship, Trail Riding and maybe Reining; or in timed events, like Barrel Racing, Pole Bending and Flag Racing. But seldom is a horse good in all events, and I don't recommend showing in all events unless your horse is trained and conditioned for them. That makes a real hard day's work, and I've seen some good horses soured from over-work.

Showmanship at halter is a fine art, which reflects months of preparation, patience and discipline of the horse and the showman (Figure 88). To some spectators, it looks simple and easy, like ballet dancing. But for the guy who consistently takes home blue ribbons (as for the ballet dancer) you can bet that it's serious business—the result of good communication with his horse, regular grooming and much practice.

GROOMING FOR FIRST PLACE

So how do you show a winner at halter? Well, if your horse is to look his Sunday best, the preparation must start months before the show with a good nutrition and health program, as described in Chapter 2. While judges say they don't like "an overly fat animal," my daughter Mary Ann and I have found that "good working condition" usually isn't enough. The horses with bloom (an extra hundred to two hundred pounds of weight) just pass us up. Even the bloomy horse, however, should have enough work or exercise to keep his muscles in tune.

To get a shining hair coat, you'll need to groom your horse every day—for at least thirty minutes—for several weeks. At every youth show, you can see horses which the owners started grooming the day before, or the week before at most. And you usually find them at the tail end of the line!

88. *Showmanship at halter is a fine art, which reflects months of preparation, patience and discipline—by horse and owner. Otherwise, your horse will not "square up and freeze" for the judge's inspection, as Kim Castor's horse is doing here.*

89. *A fresh haircut for the show. For horses with a thin neck, I prefer to leave the mane and clip the bridle path; with a thick neck, I prefer to clip the entire mane, leaving forelocks and tuft of hair on the withers.*

Bathing your horse will help (Figure 20 in Chapter 2), but don't make the mistake Mary Ann once made of giving hers a shampoo bath the night before a show. It removed the natural oil from the hair and he looked duller than ever. So if you bathe his body, do it several days before the show. Of course, you can bathe his feet, legs and face later— even on the day of the show.

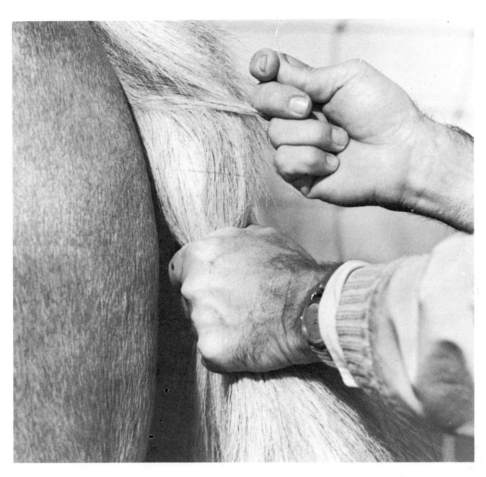

90. *Plucking or pulling the horse's tail thins the hair and makes his hips look broader. With each pull, pluck only four or five hairs—from the under side or wherever you want it thinned. Do this over a period of several days so the horse's tail and your fingers don't get sore.*

To add luster, rub him daily with a wool rag or with your hand—that is, after you use the rubber currycomb, stiff brush and soft brush. He'll look better if kept out of the sun, too, in a clean stall and covered with a blanket or sheet.

A day or two before the show, clip his bridle path (Figure 89) or mane. For horses with thick necks, I prefer to clip the entire mane,

135

91. On Quarter Horses, I prefer to thin the tail until it reaches his hocks; if shorter, it looks unnatural. But some breeds of horses show better with a long flowing tail that nearly reaches the ground.

leaving the forelocks and a tuft of hair on the withers. If you prefer a mane (I do on horses with thin necks), it should be plucked or pulled to thin it and to get the desired length. Pluck the tail the same way (Figures 90 and 91). Do this over a period of several days so the horse's tail and your hands don't get sore. Also clip the long hair on the inside and edges of the horse's ears and under the chin and jaw.

SOME FINISHING TOUCHES

Now for some finishing touches, to be performed just before you leave for the show or as soon as you arrive. Bettie Massey, one of the more experienced showmen in our 4-H Club and an AQHA Youth Champion, cleans her horse's feet with a steel brush and paints them with liquid shoe polish (Figure 92). The shoe polish is optional; most professional trainers leave it off but it does give a finished look—like fingernail polish—which girls seem to favor.

92. Bettie Massey paints the hoofs with black liquid shoe polish. Most professional trainers leave off the polish, but many girls think it adds a finished look.

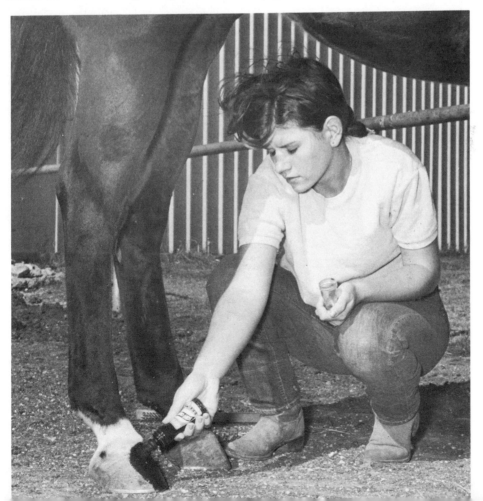

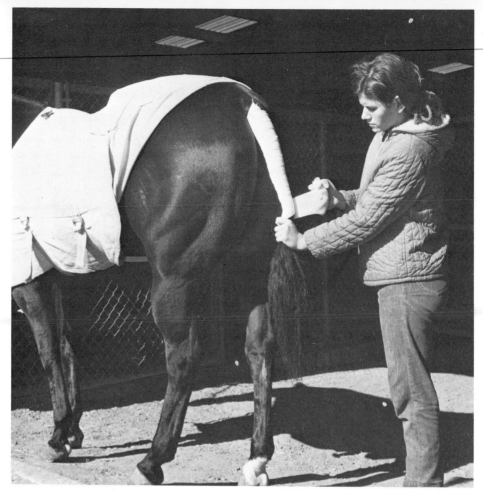

93. *To make the tail hair lie down and the horse's hips look broader, wrap the tail with an elastic knee bandage. So it won't slip down, pull up three or four hairs after each lap and cover them with the next lap. The bandage is removed, of course, before entering the show ring.*

Then Bettie dampens her horse's tail and wraps it with an elastic knee bandage (Figure 93). This makes the hairs lie down, which in turn makes the horse's hips look broader. The wrap is removed and the tail brushed just before she enters the ring. To keep the wrap from slipping down, she pulls up three to four hairs over each lap and covers them with the next lap.

Also, just before going into the ring, she sprays her horse with a "hair glow" solution containing fly repellent or wipes on the repellent. "On several occasions, one little fly has irritated Nippy and caused us to miss a blue ribbon," she declares.

138

Now Square Up and Freeze

If you've ever tried to show an untrained horse at halter, you probably wonder how some folks get their horse to square up perfectly, to stand still for long periods and to trot so willingly.

Again, let's see how Bettie Massey, who has won nearly a hundred blue ribbons at halter, does it. "It takes only five to fifteen minutes a day," she says, "but I practice squaring up Nippy every time I handle her."

In the beginning, she placed Nippy's feet with her hands (Figure 94),

94. In early training of horse to square up, Bettie Massey placed Nippy's feet with her hands. This shouldn't be necessary in the ring, however; you should control your horse completely from the halter.

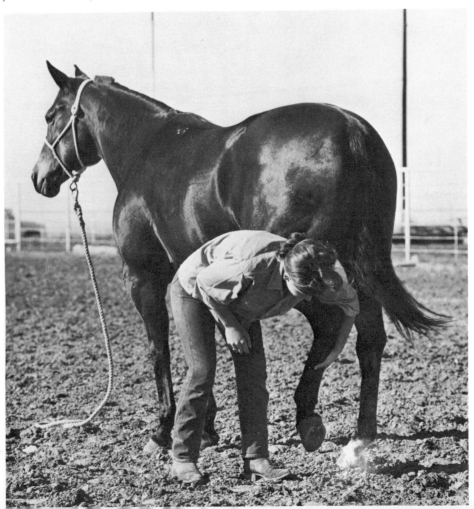

although this is frowned on by judges and shouldn't be necessary in the ring. If the horse rests her weight on one hind foot, as they do about half the time, you can even up the weight by pulling on the tail head (Figure 95) or pushing on the hip.

Next, you've got to get those front feet squared up. In training, Bettie started by using the toe of her boot (Figure 96), another practice that

95. If your horse is resting one of his rear feet, pull on his tail head to shift weight to his left foot; or push on the hip to shift weight to his right foot.

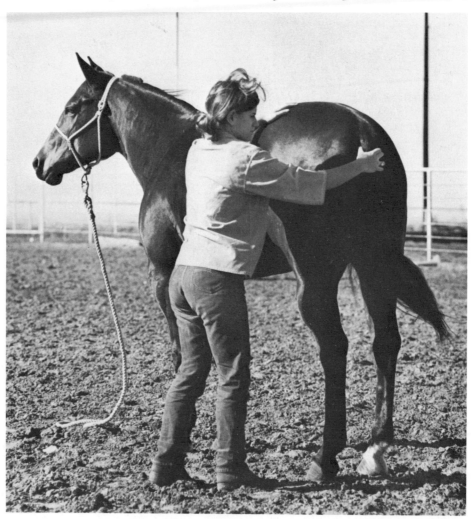

judges don't like. (Don't kick the horse on the shin; you may end up with a broken big toe.) But after enough of this training, your horse should square up in five or ten seconds, as Nippy is doing in Figure 97, without use of your hands or boot. All you should have to do to move his feet is push or pull slightly on the lead rope. And if that doesn't work, push lightly with your fingers on the horse's shoulder.

96. When training horse to square up, you may find it necessary to place his front feet with your toe. This is not good showmanship in the ring, however. There you should square up by merely pushing and pulling lightly on the halter.

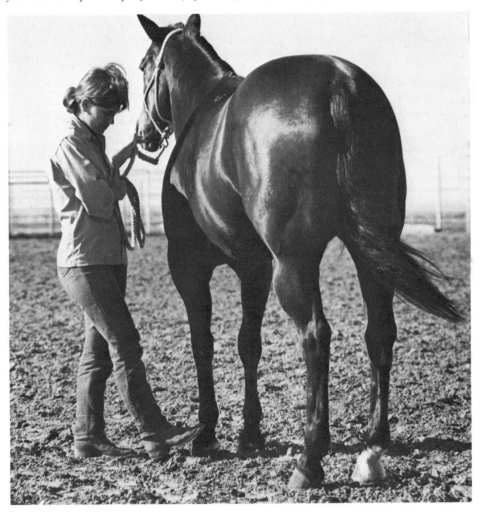

But your horse's ears won't go forward? Bettie does that finishing bit of showmanship by raising the end of her lead strap, as if she might hit her horse on the nose, and hissing (Figure 98). And indeed she does hit the horse sometimes—while training—but never in the ring.

If your horse responds well to this, you might only need to hiss or to scratch the brim of your hat to get his ears forward. George Tyler of Gainsville, Texas, one of the "winningest" professional showmen in the

97. All squared up and ready for inspection by the judge. With five to fifteen minutes of practice a day, your horse will learn to square up like this in a few seconds.

98. *To get her horse's ears forward and look alert, Bettie Massey waves end of lead strap, as if she might hit the horse, and hisses. A little of this is permissible in the show ring.*

country, says, "A horse must be a little scared of you to be alert, to give you his ears and to freeze in position." Before going into the ring, he sometimes puts a temporary lariat rope halter on his horse and gives it a few jerks. "With the rope right behind his ears, this will get his attention," assures Tyler. Of course, he puts the show halter back on before entering the ring, but the horse doesn't know that it won't hurt.

143

CLUCK AND TROT

Another part of the training, long before show day, is to teach your horse to trot—beside you, not behind you. You should walk or trot even with the horse's neck (Figure 99), which means that in the beginning

99. When showing at halter, walk and trot beside your horse's neck, not out in front of him. Do this every time you lead your horse and he'll learn to trot beside you, not behind you.

you walk by his left front leg and push forward on the lead rope with your right hand, rather than getting out in front and pulling on the rope. At first, you may have to get help from someone—to get behind the horse with a whip or to toss clods at him. Every time Bettie Massey takes her horse out of the stall she practices this and clucks at the same time. Now she merely clucks and Nippy is ready to trot as fast as Bettie wishes.

Most youth shows now have classes in Showmanship at Halter, which means that the showman is judged rather than the horse. So even if you don't have a great horse, this is one class that you can win, if you try hard. Time and again, judges and spectators say that our 4-H members do a better job of showing than most of the professional trainers, simply because they have worked at it.

Winning requires hours and hours of practice. But with practice, you can move to the front of the line, as Bettie is doing in Figure 100, and bring home a trophy.

100. In showmanship at halter, Bettie Massey moves to the head of the line again. "It's the result of a few minutes' practice—every day," she says.

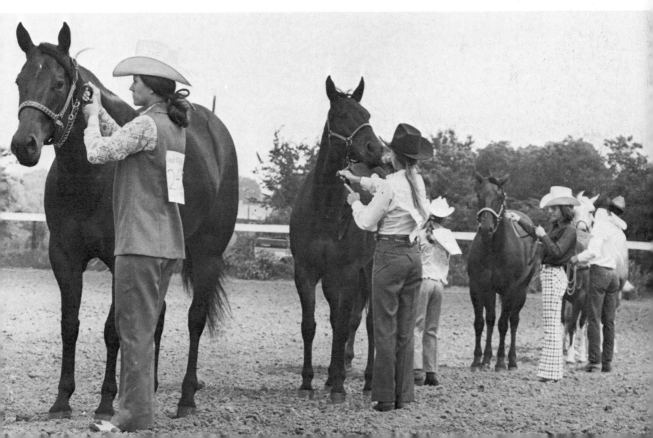

Finally, here are a few DO's and DON'Ts, based on the most common mistakes of our young showmen, that should help you:

DO wear neat, clean and appropriate dress for the class.

DON'T overshow your horse by moving excessively, waving your hands or constantly jingling the lead strap.

DO be alert, always showing your horse but keeping one eye on the judge.

DON'T get too close to the next horse and run the risk of getting kicked.

DO look happy, as if you're proud to be here and you came to win.

DON'T gripe if you fail to place. Remember that you asked the judge for his opinion and he gave it to you; good sportsmen accept it as a fair and honest verdict.

9.
Games, Contests and Horseplay

Advanced horsemanship requires a lot of work—too much work for some casual riders. They prefer to play on horses. And "horseplay" is exactly what serious horsemen call some games and contests. Personally, I think there is room for both, so long as you don't ruin a good horse by playing on him and don't play games that are unsafe.

Some contests are quite advanced, like calf roping and cutting, and require months or years of specialized training for the horse.

Others are so rough-and-tumble that they are dangerous for average young riders. That's why I don't encourage games like the Rescue Race, where one rider races to the far end of the arena, picks up a partner on the go and races back double; or the Wagon Race, where a rider pulls his partner in a "little red wagon" at high speed with a rope from the saddle horn to wagon; or the Ring Race, where riders race around the arena and spear rings hanging from a clothespin on a supporting arm. They're fast and daring, however, if that's what you want.

There are lots of other games or timed events, though, that require skill, action and speed and are relatively safe. Following are a few of the more popular ones.

BARREL RACING

Barrel racing undoubtedly is the most popular timed event for youngsters and adults. It's an event in which girls usually excel, because of

147

their lighter weight and agility. Contrary to the way you see some kids race—they just tear out, spurring, whipping and jerking their horse all the way—barrel racing really is a scientific event that requires trained skill and acute timing by horse and rider (Figure 101).

101. When approaching the barrel, aim your horse at a point about three feet to one side, check him ten or twelve feet before reaching the barrel, roll back around it, and rein him until you're in line with the next barrel. When turning to the left, horse turns on left lead, as shown here, and turns to the right on right lead.

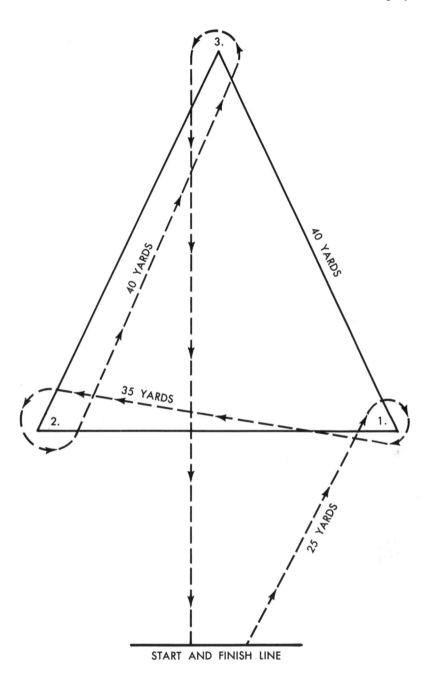

102. AGHA Barrel Race pattern.

The only equipment needed is three barrels, arranged as in Figure 102. The cloverleaf barrel pattern was originated by the Girls Rodeo Association (GRA), which calls for a spacing of 20 yards from starting line to barrel 1, 30 yards between barrels 1 and 2, and 35 yards between barrels 2 and 3. The American Quarter Horse Association (AQHA) pattern is similar but a bit longer: 25 yards from starting line to barrel 1, 35 yards to barrel 2, and 40 yards to barrel 3.

In addition, it's recommended that the starting line be 15 to 20 yards from the gate or chutes and that the barrels be at least 15 feet from the fence line and preferably 20 feet. If your arena is small and won't permit this official spacing, you can reduce the spacing between barrels 5 yards at a time, but they never should be less than 20 yards apart.

Time starts when the horse's nose crosses the starting line and ends when his nose crosses the finish line. The rules call for running around barrel 1 to the right, then around 2 and 3 to the left. Or you can reverse the pattern by running around barrel 2 to the left, then around 1 and 3 to the right. Knocking over a barrel usually calls for a five-second penalty or disqualification, depending on the show rules. Touching or holding up a barrel with your hand also will disqualify you.

"The first step in learning to run barrels is to find a suitable horse," declares Martha Josey, a champion barrel racer who also operates a barrel racing school at Karnack, Texas. "You'll need a horse that is fully seasoned—preferably eight to twelve years old—that has a good disposition, that reins well and is easy to stop. I don't believe that a young girl and a young horse can get along together. And if you can't handle him well at slow gaits, you sure can't handle him at high speeds."

After you have the right horse, Martha suggests these training and racing tips:

1. Start at a walk and a trot until your horse knows the pattern. Then gradually increase the speed.

2. Aim for a point about three feet to one side of the barrel, rather than directly at it. This will permit your horse to roll back around it, yet not make a big circle.

3. Your horse should slow down about one length before reaching the barrel and turn when—not before—you rein him. Don't release him too soon; rein him until he's in line with the next barrel.

4. Then run in a straight line, the shortest distance between two points, rather than making a big swing that requires extra steps and extra time.

5. Don't spur and whip your horse unless he starts to slow down too soon. Unnecessary use of spurs and quirt, when a horse already is doing his best, often makes him go slower.

6. Finally, don't overwork your barrel horse or he'll sour. If he's well trained, you should run the pattern very little at home. But keep him in good condition by long trotting and working him at other things for variety.

POLE BENDING

Pole Bending is another popular timed event that requires speed, good timing and smooth rhythm (Figure 103). Horses with long strides usually do best at it.

The equipment needed is six poles, 5 feet to 7 feet tall, with a heavy base (not too heavy to turn over when hit) or stakes that can be stuck in the ground. The official AQHA spacing (Figure 104) is 21 feet between poles and 21 feet to the starting line. The American Association of Sheriffs Posses and Riding Clubs (AASP&RC) rules call for 30 feet between poles, however, and 30 feet to the starting line. As with barrel racing, the time begins and ends when the horse's nose crosses the start-and-finish line.

Knocking over a pole usually results in a five-second penalty or disqualification. Touching the pole with your hand or failure to follow the prescribed pattern also calls for disqualification.

This event was my son Chuck's specialty—he and Snip won many blue ribbons in it. Snip has a long stride, changes leads smoothly and rolls back rapidly around the end poles. He weaves smoothly between poles,

103. Pole Bending is another event that requires speed, good timing and smooth rhythm. You weave between poles, so a horse that changes leads smoothly and has a long stride usually wins.

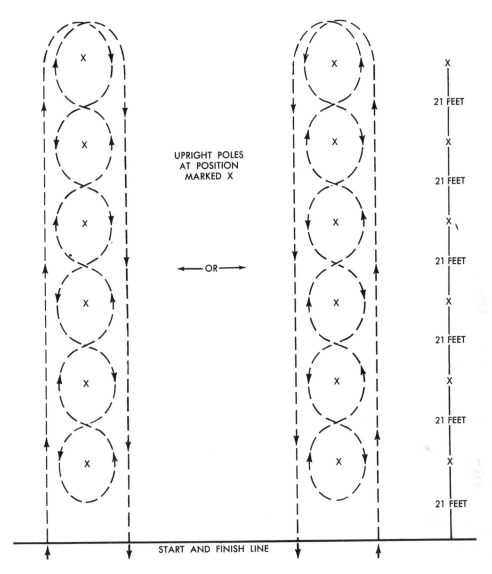

UPRIGHT POLES
AT POSITION
MARKED X

←—OR—→

21 FEET

21 FEET

21 FEET

21 FEET

21 FEET

21 FEET

21 FEET

START AND FINISH LINE

104. Pole Bending pattern.

appearing to run almost in a straight line. "A lot of good horses lose seconds because the rider reins them too much, causing wider turns and unnecessary steps," says Chuck. "Also, some riders lose out by abruptly throwing their weight to change the horse's lead. You should lean with him but stay on top and change leads with gentle reining."

153

105. *The Flag Race—a short and fast event, where you simply run to a barrel, pick up a flag as you roll back and race to the finish line—is popular among young riders.*

Flag Race

The Flag Race is a popular event among our smaller 4-H members, because it's fast—often takes less than ten seconds—and the pattern is simple. You simply run to a barrel, do a rollback around it in either direction, pick up the flag as you turn (Figure 105) and bring it back across the finish line (Figure 106).

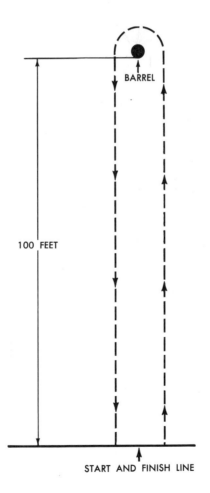

106. Flag Race pattern.

BARREL

100 FEET

START AND FINISH LINE

The only equipment needed is a barrel, a bucket of sand to hold the flag, and a small flag on a stick 12 to 15 inches long. Dropping the flag, hitting the horse with it or knocking over the barrel usually calls for disqualification.

Another version of the Flag Race, approved by the AASP&RC, is a bit more difficult (Figure 107). It requires two buckets of sand, one on each side of the arena, to hold a flag and a barrel at the far end.

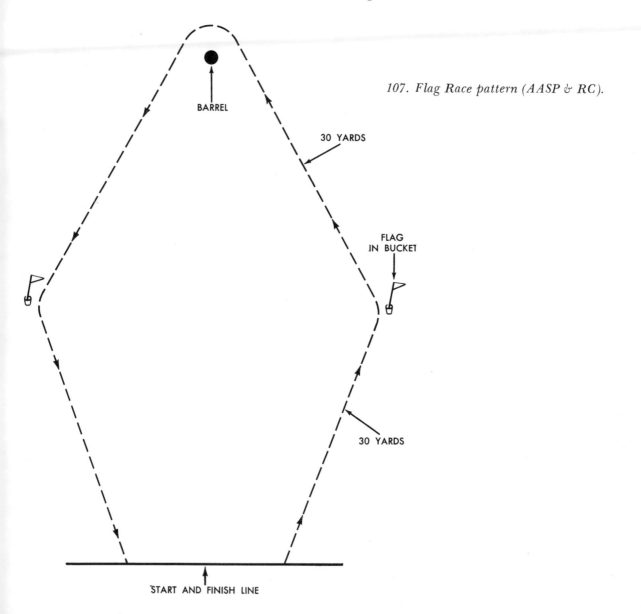

107. Flag Race pattern (AASP & RC).

BARREL

30 YARDS

FLAG
IN BUCKET

30 YARDS

START AND FINISH LINE

Here's the procedure: (1) Start with a flag in your hand. (2) Ride to the first bucket, stop and exchange flags. (3) Race around the barrel to the next bucket, stop and exchange flags. (4) Race across the finish line with the third flag in your hand.

This requires more skill and more control of your horse. It often isn't the fastest horse that wins but the one that will stop and permit you to switch flags most quickly.

STAKE RACE

The Stake Race is another simple event and is approved as an AQHA Youth Activity. It goes fast and requires very little equipment— only two poles or stakes, placed 80 feet apart, as shown in Figure 108. Around the first stake, the rider may turn either right or left so long as

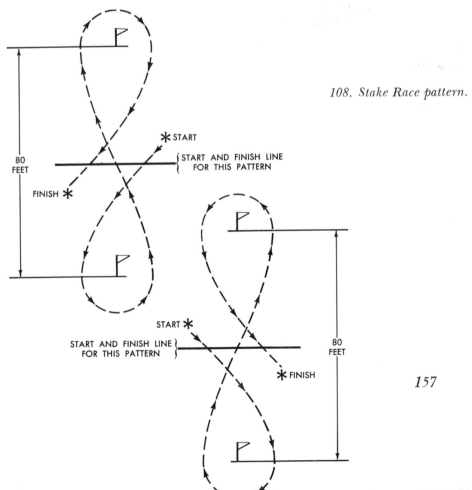

108. Stake Race pattern.

157

109. The Stake Race starts in the center of the arena, and you do a simple Figure 8 around two stakes.

he runs a Figure 8 and turns the opposite direction around the second stake (Figure 109).

QUAD-STAKE RACE

The Quad-Stake Race is another timed event, similar to the Barrel

110. The Quad-Stake Race, similar to the Barrel Race, is an unofficial timed event, but amateur riders enjoy the variety. Since the horse makes two turns to the right and two to the left, control and quick turns are just as important as speed.

Race, but it involves six markers, which may be stakes, cones or barrels (Figure 110). The pattern calls for two turns to the right and two turns to the left, with the start-and-finish line in the center as shown in Figure 111.

The four corners should be at least 15 feet from the arena fence. Knocking over a cone or stake can call for a five-second penalty or a disqualification, depending on local show rules.

159

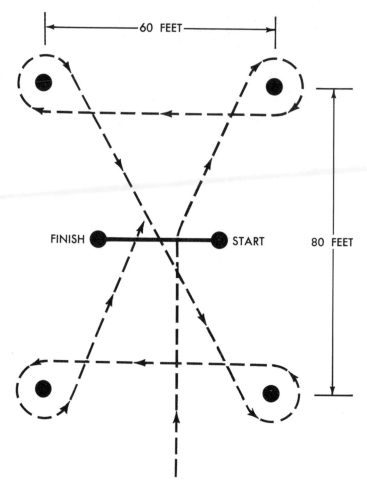

60 FEET

80 FEET

FINISH START

111. Quad-Stake Race pattern.

Keyhole Race

The Keyhole Race tests the ability of your horse to run in a straight line, stop and roll back (Figure 112). Since it's a timed event, speed is important but control of your horse is essential.

The pattern is in the shape of a keyhole with a 4-foot lane for running and a 20-foot circle for turning (Figure 113). The keyhole should

112. *The Keyhole Race, a timed event, tests the ability of your horse to run in a straight line, stop and roll back, as Melissa McMurry and Snip are doing well here.*

be marked clearly with lines of flour or lime.

If the horse steps on or over the line at any time, it's a disqualification. This is sometimes difficult to determine, so, in addition to the flagman at the start-and-finish line and timekeepers, there should be two or three officials to watch the lines for a hoofprint and to relime them.

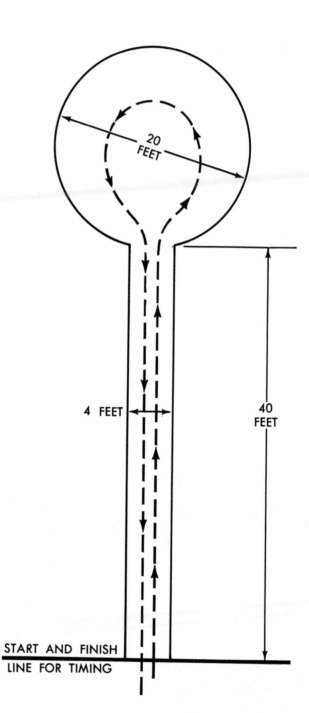

113. Keyhole Race pattern.

20
FEET

4 FEET

40
FEET

START AND FINISH
LINE FOR TIMING

POTATO RACE

For variety and laughs at your playday, try the Potato Race. Although not condoned by serious horsemen, it's a fun event that kids—from six to sixty—enjoy occasionally.

You'll need spears about 5 feet long, made of wood or light metal with a sharp point. One easy way to make them is to rip a one-inch board to get one-by-one sticks, sand the edges, drive a nail in the end and file off most of the nail head. Then you'll need a shallow wooden box, about 15 inches square, containing ten or twelve large potatoes (Figure 114).

114. A Potato Race will add variety and fun to any playday. You simply race to the box, spear a potato (if you're lucky) as you roll back (A), and race across the finish line (B). Start-and-finish line is about 150 feet from the potato box. This timed event requires a flagman and timekeeper.

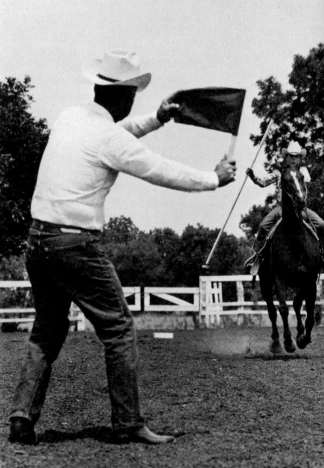

Carrying a spear, the rider crosses the start-and-finish line, races to the box (about 150 feet), pauses just long enough to spear a potato and races back with the potato on his spear. Dropping the potato or spear, of course, will disqualify him.

It's a timed event, so you'll need a flagman and timekeeper. Also, you should have an official to add a potato to the box each time one is removed, because the fewer the potatoes the harder it is to spear one.

EGG RACE

Here's an endurance race, for more laughs and fun by riders who don't have or can't ride fast horses. All they have to do is ride easy, have a steady hand and keep that egg in the spoon (Figure 115), which isn't so easy after the announcer calls for a trot and, if some riders still have their eggs, the lope. Last rider to keep his egg is the winner.

Equipment needed: A dozen tablespoons, or one spoon per rider, and an equal number of eggs. But here's a word of caution from my wife: "Mothers, don't let them take your good tablespoons, because they somehow disappear in the excitement!" Okay, then buy some 19-cent spoons for the egg race.

GOAT TIEING

To liven up our playdays, our 4-H Club has found that nothing beats Goat Tieing. Of course, the boys prefer to both rope and tie goats, but most girls can't rope them. So we sometimes stake out a goat—either a wild one or a gentle one will do—at the far end of the arena. The girls ride down near the goat, dismount, ground tie their horse, catch the goat and tie three of its feet.

115. *The Egg Race, strictly for laughs, is enjoyed by riders who don't have fast horses. Last one to keep his egg in the spoon wins.*

Time starts when they cross the starting line and ends when they finish tieing and throw up their hands. Or we sometimes vary it by having them remount and race back across the finish line, where the time ends. Of course, the goat must stay tied until they cross the finish line.

REINING CONTEST

Reining is one of the more advanced classes, which requires a well-trained horse and good horsemanship. If your horse isn't trained to do a sliding stop, back, change of leads, rollback and pivot, my advice is not to enter. (See details on these maneuvers in Chapter 5.)

If you do plan to enter Reining, make sure you know all the patterns that the judge might call for. I have seen some top horsemen, with champion horses, blow it by forgetting the pattern.

Figure 116 shows AQHA Pattern No. 1, most commonly used. You ride it thus, with numbers corresponding to numbers on the diagram: (1 to 2) Run at full speed, staying at least 20 feet from any fence or wall. (2) Stop and back. (3) Settle horse for ten seconds. (4 and 5) Ride small Figure 8 at slow canter. (6 and 7) Ride large Figure 8 fast. (8) Left rollback over hocks. (9) Right rollback over hocks. (10) Stop. (11) Pivot left or right. (12) Pivot opposite direction. (13) Walk to judge and stop for inspection until dismissed.

The AQHA has four standard reining patterns, which you can get from the AQHA Rule Book. But at the National Reining Horse Futurity in Ohio, the judges dream up additional patterns, which they reveal to riders only the night before. This means that your horse should be trained to do any maneuver upon call and should not memorize any one pattern. For this reason, the best trainers do not practice a regular pattern at home; otherwise, the horse might anticipate it and "set up" in competition.

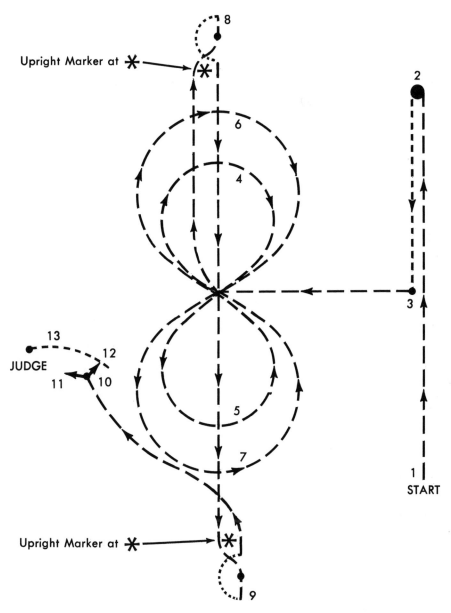

Upright Marker at ✳

Upright Marker at ✳

116. AQHA Reining Pattern No. 1.

WESTERN RIDING HORSE CONTEST

The Western Riding Horse Contest is a true measure of pleasure horses. It's designed to check the performance of a sensible, well-man-

117. *The Western Riding Horse Contest requires a sensible, well-mannered horse, the kind needed for ranch chores. While zigzagging through cones, the horse must pass over a log without breaking gait.*

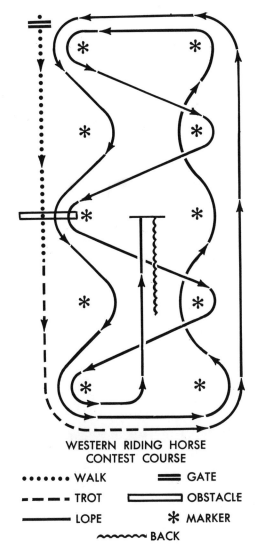

WESTERN RIDING HORSE
CONTEST COURSE

•••••• WALK   ══ GATE

-- -- - TROT   ▭ OBSTACLE

——— LOPE   ✻ MARKER

〜〜〜 BACK

118. Western Riding pattern.

nered, free and easy-moving ranch horse—the kind to get a man around on the usual ranch chores (Figure 117).

In addition to the walk, trot, lope, change of leads, stop and back, it includes opening and closing a gate and passing over a log, which causes some horses to break gait (Figure 118).

Trail Horse Class

The Trail Horse Class is one of the most varied and difficult for pleasure horses. It is judged 10 percent on conformation of the horse, 30 percent on his rail work (walk, trot and lope) and 60 percent on his work over the obstacles.

While there is no prescribed course, six obstacles are required by the AQHA. The three mandatory obstacles are: (1) opening, passing through and closing a gate (Figure 119), (2) riding over at least four logs and (3) riding over a wooden bridge.

119

Then three of the following optional obstacles are performed: (1) Ride through a ditch of water or shallow pond. (2) Hobble or ground tie your horse. (3) Carry an object (like a sack of feed) from one part of the arena to another. (4) Back through an L-shaped course. (5) Put on and remove slicker. (6) Dismount and lead your horse over obstacles 14 to 24 inches high. (7) Send your horse freely into a horse trailer (see Chapter 10).

If you think these are easy, as some riders do, then try the obstacles that the Appaloosa Horse Club adds to some trail classes: Walk over a seesaw bridge with two flapping geese tied by the feet and slung over your saddle. Drag a stiff cowhide toward your horse and up over the saddle. Or load your horse into a stock trailer with a squealing pig! It's a real test of how your horse might cope with unexpected hazards on the range.

119. For opening and closing a gate, a requirement in several classes, you need a calm trained horse that responds to leg pressure. Properly done, you (A) open gate, (B) pass through and (C) close and latch gate without changing rein hands and without taking your hand off the gate.

10.
Trailers and Trailering

You hear a lot of cracks these days about folks with "a hundred-dollar horse and a thousand-dollar trailer." But as a friend told me recently, "If you can't afford a trailer, you've got no business with a horse. It's almost as essential as a saddle."

Well, my friend has been known to exaggerate a bit, but not much this time. A trailer will open up a much wider world for you and your horse, permitting you to travel with him, attend shows, make trail rides and even take him on vacation with you. Because so many folks do travel with their horses, "horse motels" are springing up across the country, and there now is a horse motel directory.

MANY KINDS OF TRAILERS

What kind of trailer for you? They vary all the way from $200 open-stock trailers to $5,000 enclosed semi-van trailers. We started with a $100 used stock trailer, which served our purpose as long as we had only one horse and were traveling short distances, but have since graduated to a two-horse tandem axle trailer, the kind that is most popular now.

While there are many kinds and models of trailers, the three main types (Figure 120) are (1) the two-horse tandem, (2) the two-horse in-line and (3) the four-horse gooseneck.

120. Three popular types of trailers, from left: (1) Two-horse tandem-axle has four wheels and is easy to back. (2) Two-horse in-line puts no weight on your car and is more stable but costs more. (3) Four-horse gooseneck puts weight on pickup ahead of rear axle; thus is easier to pull and corner sharply.

The two-horse tandem trailer has four wheels, which makes it easy and safe to pull, even at high speeds. These vary in price from $800 for stripped models to $2,000 for deluxe models. Even the stripped models should have lights and turn signals. And if you're going to haul much, I think your trailer should have brakes, either electric or hydraulic. I prefer electric brakes, which add $100 to $200 to the cost, but they are simple and safe. My trailer brakes are automatically connected when I connect the lights. And I can vary the amount of braking on the trailer, depending on the load, with a simple control under the steering wheel.

After that, the extras—escape doors (Figure 121), rubber floor mats, feeding door, pads to protect your horse, saddle rack in the tack storage compartment (Figure 122), interior lights, vents, curtains for bad weather and even dressing rooms in the super deluxe models—simply depend on your taste and your pocketbook.

121. Escape doors are not for your escape after leading horse into trailer; they really are access doors for tieing your horse or helping him when in trouble.

175

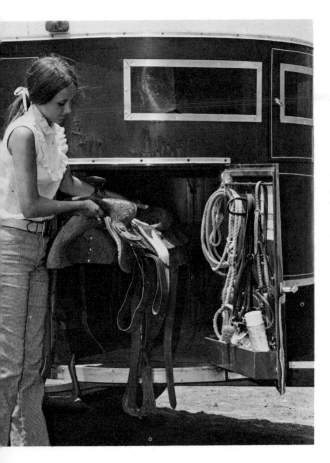

122. The tack compartment in front of our tandem trailer is handy and always full—of saddles, bridles, ropes, grooming equipment and feed. Sliding saddle rack, which holds two saddles, and lock on the door are especially convenient.

The rubber floor mats (made of old tires) and escape doors really aren't luxuries. The mats will keep your horse from slipping and, if you're hauling long distances, cushion the vibration and make the trip much easier on him. The escape doors, despite their name, aren't in-

123. *Rump chain is to hold horse in trailer while you close and fasten door. This full partition keeps horses completely separated but causes some horses to lose their footing and scramble.*

tended to provide an escape after you walk into the trailer with your horse behind you. (That's not the way to load a horse—it's dangerous—because the horse might lunge forward and pin you.) They're really access doors, for reaching the horse to tie him or to help him in case of trouble.

You will want a partition between horses and a rump chain (Figure 123) to hold them in until you can close the door after loading. The

124. A partial partition permits horses to spread their feet and ride more securely. Trainers who haul horses a lot prefer this.

partition can be full (Figure 123) or partial (Figure 124). We have an old roping horse, Rock, that tries to spread out over two thirds of the trailer. With a full partition, he scrambles and kicks and sometimes gets down. But with a partial partition, which can be a ten-inch board or a two-inch pipe, he can spread his feet out and be hauled calmly.

If you're sure you'll never haul more than one horse, a single-horse tandem trailer is adequate and about $200 cheaper. But sooner or later, most of us want to haul a second horse, either for a friend or another of our own.

The four-wheel in-line trailers, where one horse stands behind the other, are gaining in popularity. They have several advantages: (1) They are more stable and safer at high speeds, because they have two wheels in front and two in back, like an auto. (2) They put no weight on the car and thus are easier to pull. And (3) the horses haul better, because each stall is about six inches wider.

But in-line trailers have a couple of disadvantages; First, they cost about $1,000 more than a tandem. (Two-horse models list for $2,000 to $3,500; similar four-horse models cost about $3,000 to $4,000). And second, they are harder to back.

For hauling four horses, the new gooseneck trailers, pulled by a pickup, seem to be the best. The weight on the pickup is just ahead of the rear axle, so there is no weaving at high speeds and you can turn them short like a semi-trailer truck. Cost, $2,000 to $4,500.

If you are using an open stock trailer, I suggest that you get some plastic goggles to cover your horse's eyes, especially if you're hauling at night. A leather shop can make them, if you can't buy ready-made ones, for $5 to $10. We used to put goggles on our horse when we had an open trailer, and got a lot of compliments for good care.

You'll need a strong, safe hitch on your car, especially for the tandem trailer. "The hitch height, which varies for different trailers, is critical," says S. B. Miley of the Miley Trailer Company, largest horse trailer manufacturer in the country. "When the trailer is loaded it should be level, or the front end slightly higher. If the rear of your car is depressed and the trailer is tilted downward, you're pulling a potential accident!"

This means that you'll probably need some heavy duty springs or shock absorbers on your car. I prefer air shocks, in which I can vary the pressure from zero to ninety pounds and thus raise or lower the hitch height.

TEACHING A HORSE TO LOAD

As a 4-H Club leader, I haul a lot of horses for our members, and occasionally a kid says something like, "Sweety just doesn't like to load." Fact is, nobody has taken the time to train Sweety to load. Or she has been hurt or mistreated in loading. And I'll admit, when you're hauling a hitchhiking horse, you're usually in a hurry and don't have much patience with Sweety.

Like everything else with horses, training to load takes time and patience. Of course a horse is afraid to go into that strange little box the first time. It helps to park the trailer next to a barn or fence so he can't walk around it (Figure 125). Then you should talk to him, reassure him, give him time to see and smell what's in the trailer. My daughter Mary Ann has coaxed spooky horses into trailers with feed. First, she sets the feed bucket near the trailer, then barely in it, and gradually moves it up until the horse is in and eating.

125. In teaching horse to load or in loading a problem horse, it helps to place trailer near a barn or fence so he can't walk around it. Talk to him, reassure him, give him time to see and smell that strange little box.

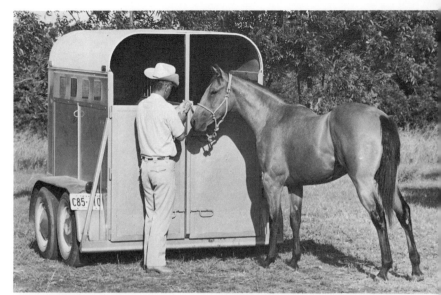

126. Teaching a horse to load. One good way is: (A) Tie him to a trailer for an hour or two a day for two or three days. (B) Then open door and tie him so he can get in or out. (C) He'll soon get inquisitive and get in—on his own.

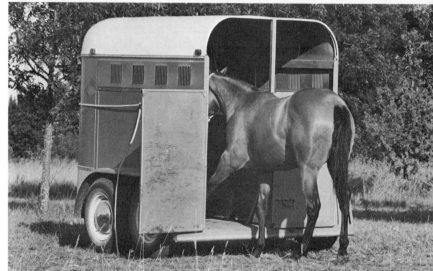

A neighbor of ours has an old trailer sitting on the ground, without wheels or doors, and feeds his yearling colts in it. "They get to where they'll almost run over you to get in a trailer," he claims.

Davidson, my trainer friend, uses another method that he says has never failed. He ties the young horse to the back of the trailer for an hour or two at a time. After two or three days of this, the horse learns that the trailer isn't going to hurt him. Then Davidson leaves the trailer door open and ties the horse with a long lead rope, which is run through the feed door and back to the side of the trailer.

"Because a young horse is inquisitive, he'll explore," explains Davidson. "First, he'll put his front feet up in the trailer and back out a few times. Then he'll go all the way—on his own." This training takes a few days, but it seems to work for both young horses and old horses (Figure 126).

LOADING A PROBLEM HORSE

If you're picking up a friend's crazy old nag and you're running late for a show, you may have a problem. Three times out of four, I find that a rope—I always carry a lariat rope in the trailer—over his hips will get the job done (Figure 127). If he's gentle, two men with hands clasped behind his rump usually can push him in (Figure 128).

Sometimes an old broomtail will get his front feet in the trailer and go no farther. A swat on the rump with your hand or a rope will usually finish the job, but it sometimes causes him to make a hasty retreat. In this case, I just put my shoulder against his rump and push him in (Figure 129). That failing, I tie one end of the rope to the side of the trailer, run it around his rump, loop it around the center post of the trailer a couple of times and give him a hard swat.

These emergency methods aren't necessary if the horse has been properly trained, but it's one way to get on to the show. In fact, I don't

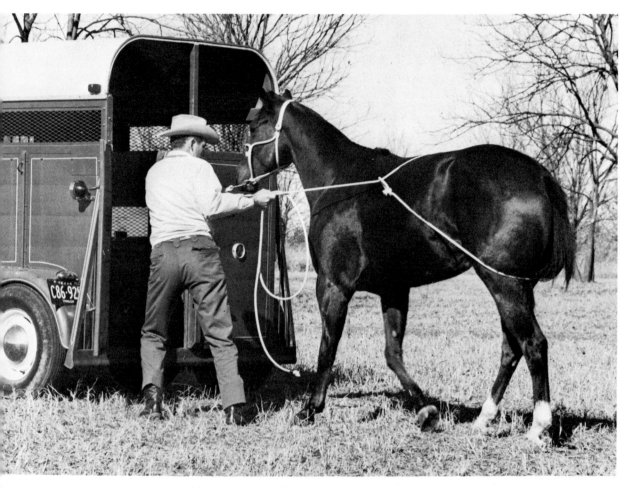

127. *When loading a problem horse in a hurry, I find that a loop over the rump usually will move a horse forward and into the trailer. This is recommended only for horses that you are hauling one time and don't have time to train.*

like to use ropes on my own horses because they'll soon get to relying on the ropes.

183

128. *If horse is reluctant to go all the way in a trailer, two men with hands clasped behind his rump usually can push him in.*

129. *If a gentle horse gets halfway in trailer and balks, I simply lean against his rump and push him in. Another way, which really is safer, is to tie the long rope so he can't back out, and swat him with a whip.*

HAULING HORSES

After your horses are loaded, hauling usually is no problem, *if you are a careful driver and anticipate possible dangers*. Take precautions to start slowly, turn corners easily and brake gently; otherwise, the horse can lose his footing and become excited.

If your horse tends to scramble, wrapping his legs will help prevent injury, usually caused from stepping on himself or kicking. Use cotton padding under the wraps and don't wrap tightly enough to reduce circulation. Another thing that will help is a partial partition (see Figure 124) so he can spread out his feet.

Some horses, especially stallions, just won't haul calmly beside another horse. In which case, your best bet is to get a single horse trailer or an in-line trailer. But if you must haul an excitable stallion beside another horse, try placing Vicks salve in his nostrils so he can't smell anything else. It often works!

Hauling mares and foals can be a problem, too. You'll want to take every precaution to prevent the mare from stepping on the foal, if it becomes tired and lies down. The best way, if you have or can borrow a stock trailer with front and back compartments, is to put the foal up front and the mare in back so she can see her baby.

Two final reminders on hauling: Inspect your trailer occasionally for sharp corners or objects. Otherwise, you might arrive at a show, as one of our club members did recently, and find that your horse has a bloody face. And just before pulling out, always check to make sure that your trailer is hitched securely, all the doors are fastened and the tires are up.

11.
Trouble Shooting

If a horse is trained properly, he isn't likely to have many bad habits. But sooner or later, we all end up with a horse that "the other fellow has spoiled." Then we have to try to correct the problem.

Through the years, the thirty-five members in our 4-H Club have had about every problem imaginable. When I didn't know the solution or when my "solution" didn't work, we have consulted various trainers. Here are some of the members' more common problems and questions and the best answers that we have found.

"My horse is barn sour. Every time I ride near the barn he wants to go to it and I can hardly turn him away."

He probably got barn sour because you or somebody else has loped him up to the barn and gotten off. Try riding him a lot in front of the barn, not letting him stop there. When you're through, ride him away from the barn, stop, get off and lead him back. Always stop headed away from the barn and lead him back.

"When I tie my horse, he occasionally rears back and breaks the reins. What can I do, because I must tie him at times?"

Bridle reins weren't made for tieing a horse. Even if he is gentle, you should tie him with a halter and strong lead rope to a secure object. (See Figure 26 in Chapter 3.)

If your horse rears back, even when tied with a halter, there are two ways of possibly breaking him. Some trainers loop a rope around the

130. *To break a horse from rearing back when tied, run a rope (with slip loop) around his girth, through his front legs, through the halter ring and tie it high to a tree. When he rears back, the rope will tighten around his girth, causing him to lunge forward.*

188

horse's girth, then run the end between his front legs, through the halter, and tie it high to a tree (Figure130). To make sure the horse rears back, they then "sack out" the horse by putting a feed sack over a broom and rubbing it all over the horse. When he does pull back, the loop tightens around his girth and makes him lunge forward.

Other trainers do it slightly differently—by tieing the rope to the horse's front foot, through the halter and to a tree. Now when the horse pulls back, he pulls his foot off the ground and will lunge forward.

"My mare sometimes bites me. It usually doesn't hurt, but sometimes it does. Should I punish her?"

You bet. Hit her as soon as possible with the closest thing available. Don't just peck, hit her hard enough to hurt because she can hurt you. Don't feed her out of your hand and never show your love by rubbing your face against the horse's nose.

"My horse won't back. No matter how hard I tug on the reins, he just bows his neck and plants his feet. Can you teach an old horse to back?"

Tugging on the reins won't do it. It's easier to teach a young horse to back, although you can teach an old one. In either case, start on the ground by pushing him back and commanding, "Back, back." (See Figure 44 in Chapter 4.) If necessary, tap him on the chest with a quirt or stick until he backs one or two steps. Then stop and reward him by stroking his neck. The next day, make him back three or four steps and increase it a little each day.

After he has learned to back with you on the ground, mount him and follow a similar procedure. You may need a friend to help you with the stick, as in Figure 45 in Chapter 4. But before asking him to back, make sure he is collected; put your weight in the stirrups so he can bend his back a little; take the reins in both hands and pull gently. Don't tug; apply slight pressure and release, slight pressure and release.

"My horse likes to chew on wood; he just eats up the board fences and stable doors. Is this bad for the horse and what can I do?"

Chewing on wood isn't necessarily harmful to the horse, but it's a nuisance and can lead to cribbing or wind sucking, which is more serious. A wind sucker clamps his teeth on a board and sucks in air, audibly.

This usually happens to horses that are confined or inactive over long periods. They're simply bored or frustrated. So the best prevention is a vigorous daily workout. If you can't ride him every day, take fifteen or twenty minutes to exercise him on a longe line (Figure 46 in Chapter 4). Professional trainers with a number of horses often use a mechanical exerciser, which permits them to exercise up to six horses at a time.

If your horse already has the habit, changing his quarters, providing a larger exercise area and feeding adequate roughage may help. Painting the boards with creosote often helps, too.

"What causes a horse to weave, to stand in the stall and shift his weight from foot to foot like an elephant?"

Again, he's bored and needs regular exercise. Some trainers relieve this boredom by putting a goat in the stall with the horse. Nervous horses like company and usually will take up with a goat or even with a chicken. Other trainers hang a tether ball from the ceiling, about head high, which gives the nervous horse something to play with rather than weave.

"When I ride, my horse gapes his mouth as if he is trying to spit out the bit. I'm not pulling hard on the reins. Should I change bits?"

Yes, try other bits. But don't go and buy a bunch of bits; maybe you can borrow different kinds until you find one that doesn't aggravate him. Chances are that your current bit is hurting him or he has been hurt with an earlier bit. Work with him gently, trying to get response with an easy touch and soft talk.

Some trainers tie the horse's mouth shut with a wire or strap (Figure 131) and then are very careful not to pull hard on the reins. Otherwise, they would hurt his mouth even more and cause him to rear. If you try this, first work him on the ground a while, because some horses become excited and rear when their mouth is tied shut.

131. When horse gapes mouth, it usually means the bit is irritating him. If changing bits doesn't help, some trainers tie mouth shut with a strap or wire.

"I have a new horse that rears up a lot. Hitting him over the head doesn't help. What can I do?"

Your horse probably is mad, and hitting him over the head can make matters worse. Try calming him by placing your hand on his head and talking to him. If you can get him to backing, rather than rearing, it'll help. Some trainers spin a horse until he gets dizzy, as punishment for rearing, and this discourages it; he can't rear when he's spinning. Also, you might try another bit; your present bit may be hurting him.

"My horse won't stand still for mounting. He's not a high horse, but he just walks off when I start to mount."

He's spoiled. If you mount properly (see Figure 74 in Chapter 7), you can take up on the reins and make him "whoa" immediately. Get him in the habit of standing still for a minute or so every time you mount.

If you are too small to mount easily, you might hobble your horse (Figure 37 in Chapter 4) or tie him to a fence. Then get on and off until he doesn't mind and stands still.

"My horse won't pivot properly; he turns on his front feet instead of his hind feet."

You probably are letting him go forward when you turn around, rather than pulling him back diagonally until his hind feet are under him (Figure 132).

Some trainers, when working an old horse that never has been taught to pivot, will turn him into a log or stack of crossties. If he doesn't get back, he'll bump his shins. Still other trainers use a fence or barn (Figure 56 in Chapter 5).

You might get the habit of backing your horse two or three steps every time you stop (Figure 42 in Chapter 4). This will help him get his hind

132. *To pivot properly, a horse must have his hind feet well under him. When turning 180 degrees, get your horse in the habit of turning on his hind feet rather than walking around on his front feet. Keep reins low and pull them diagonally in the direction horse is to pivot.*

193

133. *If the horse is too large for you to saddle and bridle from the ground, use a box or platform. To help small boys and girls, Ranchland, Inc., a horse camp in Texas, has narrow stalls with an elevated walkway on each side of horse.*

feet under; then when they're under, turn him.

Don't tug and try to pull your horse around with strength. As in all training, take it easy, be patient, show him what you want and practice every day.

"My horse is spooky. He shies from the most insignificant little things. Should I whip him?"

No, whipping probably would make him worse. He could have bad eyesight, but chances are he simply is scared and needs reassurance. Stop him, talk to him, ease him up to the object and pet him. Also, you might expose him to more of the things that scare horses, like noise, traffic, horns, lights, people and other horses. Get him accustomed to these things before you try to show him so you won't be embarrassed.

Likewise, when crossing ditches or climbing banks, ease your horse across them. Make him walk across rather than jump. It's all a part of getting your horse under control and training him to do exactly what you want him to do.

"My horse is hard to bridle. Sometimes he won't take the bit unless I force it into his mouth."

Chances are that forcing the bit into his mouth has hurt his gums and causes him to refuse the bit. (See the proper way to bridle, Figure 31 in Chapter 3.) Other causes are putting a hot bit (from lying in the sun) or a cold bit (warm the mouthpiece with your hand) into his mouth.

If your horse won't open his mouth, slip your thumb into the side of his mouth—on the bar or roof where there are no teeth—and press until he does open. Still another way, which some kids use successfully, is to put honey or molasses on the mouthpiece. Horses like the sweet taste and in two or three days will welcome the sweet bit.

If he raises his head too high for you and if you use a tiedown, put the tiedown on first. Or you can use a box or platform (Figure 133).

195

"When changing leads, my horse will change in front but won't change his hind lead. Can this be corrected?"

This is called cross-leading or being disunited (Figure 53 in Chapter 5). The problem is that you or somebody has let the horse cross-lead, which is unnatural and awkward, until it has become comfortable for him. First, make sure that you know the leads; then, if he starts off wrong, stop him immediately and correct him. Work him in small circles—on the correct leads—until they become comfortable and natural for him.

Now if he continues to drag the hind lead, try tapping him on the leg that is off lead with a long piece of baling wire. This should cause him to draw it up into the correct position. If he responds to this, use the ends of your reins to tap him and later just raise your hand or elbow.

"My horse is too fast for Western Pleasure classes. Is there any way to slow him down?"

You may need to get him tired before the class; at least, ride him enough to get the edge off. At home, ride him a lot in the slow lope—pull him down and talk to him. Of course, some horses can't be slowed down enough to win in Western Pleasure and should be used for something else.

"My horse won't neck rein. When turning or loping in circles, he turns his head outward, rather than in the direction we're going."

A lot of beginning riders have this problem and don't know it. Your horse should turn his head in the direction you're turning—look where he's going—so his neck and body form an arc that coincides with the circle that you are attempting to follow. (See Figures 134 and 135.)

196

134. Incorrect reining, demonstrated by Darrell Davidson. Horse is loping in a circle to the left but has his head turned to the right. A lot of riders have this problem and don't know it. To correct, pull reins diagonally to the left rear and tighten up left rein as in the next picture.

If your horse is trained properly and is reined properly, he'll do it. But riders sometimes overdo it. They attempt to neck rein to the left, for example, and pull so hard or so far left that the right rein becomes tighter and pulls the horse's head to the right (wrong direction). If this is happening to you, try pulling the reins back more—diagonally to the left and rear—rather than 90 degrees to the left.

197

135. *When horse is circling, his neck should be arced and pointed in the direction of travel. Practice this for two or three days at the walk, then the trot and lope. In teaching a horse to rein, most professionals use two hands on the reins.*

If this doesn't work, take the reins in both hands, lay the right rein against his neck, go down the left rein with your left hand and pull his head to the left. Do this at the walk (for two or three days), trot and canter—to the left and right—until he responds to the cue of the rein against his neck. By the way, most trainers use two hands on the reins when training, even on old horses.

136. When training a horse to ground tie or to longe, trainer Dwight Stewart uses a war bridle attached to a long rope. Smooth chain runs from left ring on noseband, over the poll, through right ring on noseband and back through left ring. It can be severe but gives good control of horse. See Photo 137.

137. *Teaching horse to ground tie, Dwight Stewart takes long rope in hand, tells horse to "Whoa," and steps around corner so horse can't see him. If horse moves, he gives a slight jerk on rope until horse learns to stand still.*

"My horse has a tough mouth and is hard to handle. Should I change bits?"

When young horses are first bitted, nearly all of them have a soft or tender mouth. It may become tough or cold from abuse, because someone jerks on the reins and damages the nerves; or because someone is heavy-handed and rides constantly with a tight rein. So the cause of a tough mouth usually is the rider. Try to train your horse so he will respond to cues and light reining.

If his mouth already is damaged, you may need a more severe bit—a higher port, a spade or a longer shank. If you still have trouble, you might try a hackamore bit. But if your horse doesn't perform because you can't handle him, a hackamore probably won't solve the problem.

"Some riders can get off their horse, drop the reins and the horse stands still. How can I teach my horse to ground tie?"

Here are three ways that I have seen work: The first is to start in a small pen and talk to your horse, saying "Whoa," while walking around him or away from him. The second is to hobble him (Figure 37 in Chapter 4) until he learns to stand still. Some cowboys continue to do this in pastures, even with old horses. The third is to use a war bridle and long rope to remind the horse that he must stand, even when you are out of sight (Figures 136 and 137). You go around the corner or inside the feed room; then if the horse starts to move, give the rope a slight jerk and call "Whoa." In all cases, as with all horse training, it takes days of practice, practice.

12.
Talk Like a Horseman

AGED: A term indicating that the horse is ten years of age or older.

AIDS: The legs, hands, weight and voice, as they are used to control a horse.

APPALOOSA: A breed of horses, developed by the Nez Percé Indians, with a blanket of white over the hips or with egg-shaped spots. All Appaloosas have white circles around the eye and hoofs with vertical black and white stripes.

APPOINTMENTS: Equipment and clothing used in showing.

BARREN MARE: A mare that is not in foal; infertile.

BEARING REIN: Neck rein; rein pushed against neck in direction of turn.

BIT: The metal part of the bridle that fits in the horse's mouth.

BLEMISH: Any mark or deformity that diminishes beauty but does not affect usefulness.

BLOOM: A term usually applied to a fat horse with hair that is clean and glossy.

BOSAL: That part of the hackamore that fits over the nose.

BRIDLE: The headgear used to control a horse. Usually consists of a headstall, bit and reins.

BROOMTAIL: A Western range horse; a poor, ill-kept horse of uncertain breed.

BUCK-KNEED: Knees bent forward.

BUG-EYED: Eyes protruding; horse usually cannot see well.

CALF-KNEED: Knees bent backward, the opposite of buck-kneed.

CANNON: The lower leg bone below knee and hock. See Figure 5.

CANTER: A three-beat gait, a lope, a collected gallop.

CANTLE: The back of a saddle. See Figure 68.

CASTRATION: Removal of testicles from a male. A castrated male horse is a gelding.

CHAPS, CHAPARAJOS: Seatless overalls made of leather and worn over jeans for protection when riding in brush or in cold weather.

CHESTNUTS: The horny growths on the inside of a horse's leg; also called night eyes. See Figure 5.

COARSE: Lacking refinement; a rough, harsh appearance.

COLLECTED: A horse that's alert, at attention, with his feet properly under him.

COLT: A young male horse. Sometimes used to describe any young horse.

CONFORMATION: The build of a horse—the structure, form and symmetrical arrangement of parts.

COON-FOOTED: Long sloping pasterns throwing fetlocks low.

COW-HOCKED: Hocks close together, feet wide apart.

CREST: Upper, curved part of neck, peculiar to stallions.

CRIBBING: Biting or setting teeth against manger or some other object while sucking air.

CROUP: Part of the back just in front of base of tail. See Figure 5.

DAM: The female parent of a horse.

DEFECT: Any mark or flaw that impairs usefulness; unsoundness.

DISUNITED: When a horse is on the right front lead and left hind lead or vice versa. Also called *cross-leading*. See Chapter 5.

DRESSAGE: Advanced training or intricate maneuvers without audible commands or visible signals.

EQUINE: Of or pertaining to a horse.

EQUITATION: Art of horsemanship. In equitation events, the rider and not the horse is judged.

ERGOT: A horny growth behind the fetlock joint.

EWE-NECKED: Top profile of neck (just in front of withers) concave like a female sheep's neck.

FARRIER: A horseshoer.

FAR SIDE: The right side of a horse.

FAVOR: To spare or protect; to limp slightly.

FENDERS: The wide pieces of leather along the stirrup leather. See Figure 68.

FETLOCK: A projection on the lower part of the leg of a horse, above and behind the hoof. See Figure 5.

FILLY: A female horse up to three years, the age at which she becomes a mare.

FIVE-GAITED: A saddle horse trained to perform in five gaits—the walk, trot, canter, rack (single-foot) and one of the slow gaits (running walk, fox trot, or stepping pace).

FLOATING: Filing of rough, irregular teeth to give a smoother grinding surface.

FOAL: Colt or filly under one year old.

FOUNDER: To stumble and go lame; also, an inflammation of the feet, causing lameness.

FOX TROT: A slow, short, shuffling gait, where the hind foot strikes the ground an instant before the diagonal front foot.

FROG: The triangular pad in the sole of a horse's foot.

GAIT: The manner of going. The straight gaits are walk, trot, canter and gallop; the slow gaits are running walk, fox trot and stepping pace.

GALLOP: A three-beat gait resembling the canter but faster (twelve miles per hour) or a long lope.

GASKIN: The muscular part of the hind leg above the hock. See Figure 5.

GELD: To cut or castrate a male horse, making him infertile.

GELDING: An altered or castrated horse.

GESTATION PERIOD: The length of time from breeding to birth of foal, usually about eleven months.

GET: The progeny of a stallion.

GIRTH OR GIRT: The corded piece or leather strap that fits under the horse's stomach to hold the saddle in place; also, the circumference of a horse's body back of the withers.

GLASS EYE: A blue or whitish eye.

GOOSE-RUMPED: Having narrow, drooping rump.

GREEN HORSE: One with little training.

GROOM: To clean and brush a horse; also, the person who does this.

HACKAMORE: A bitless bridle of various designs used in breaking and training. See Figures 59 and 67.

HAND: A unit of measure equal to four inches. Horses are measured from withers to ground in hands. See Figure 6.

HEADSTALL: The leather bridle straps, exclusive of bit and reins.

HOBBLE: Strap or rope fastened to the front legs of a horse to prevent him from straying from camp. See Figure 37.

HOCK: The tarsal joint of the hind leg of a horse, corresponding to the human ankle. See Figure 5.

HORSE: An animal measuring more than 14.2 hands (58 inches); also, a general term for any horse.

HORSE LENGTH: Eight feet, the distance between horses in a column.

HORSEMANSHIP: Art of riding the horse and of understanding his needs.

JACK: A male donkey or ass.

JOCKEY: The leather flaps on the side of a saddle. See Figure 68.

LEAD: The foot that moves out farther in the lope or canter. A horse may travel on his left lead or right lead.

LEAD STRAP: A strap or rope attached to the halter for leading.

LIGHT HORSE: Any horse used primarily for riding or driving; all breeds except draft breeds.

LONGE: A long line, about twenty to thirty feet, used in training and exercising a horse. See Figure 46.

LOPE: A three-beat gait, a canter, a collected gallop.

MARE: A mature female horse, three years old or over.

MARTINGALE: A strap running from the girth between the front legs to the bridle. The standing martingale is attached to the bit. The running martingale has rings through which the reins pass. See Figure 63.

MULE: A cross between a jack and a mare.

NEAR SIDE: The horse's left side.

OFF SIDE: The horse's right side.

OUTFIT: The equipment of a horseman; tack.

OUTLAW: A horse that cannot be broken.

PACE: An artificial gait in which the two legs on the same side of the horse move forward at the same time.

PASTERN: The part of a horse's foot between the fetlock and hoof. See Figure 5.

PINTO or PAINT: A horse with white and colored spots over the body. There are two color patterns—*overo,* where the primary color is dark with white spots, and *tobiana,* where white is the primary color with a secondary dark color.

POLL: The top of a horse's head just back of the ears.

PONY: A horse measuring 14.2 hands or less at the withers.

PORT: The part of the mouthpiece of a bit curving up over the tongue.

POSTING: The rising and descending of a rider, through knee action, with the rhythm of the trot.

PROUD CUT: A term indicating that castration was improperly performed. The gelding acts like a stallion but is infertile.

PULLED TAIL: A tail thinned by pulling hairs. See Figure 90.

RACK: An artificial gait in which the horse's feet hit the ground one at at time in a steady one-two-three-four sequence, similar to the walk but with a higher and faster action. Also called *single-foot.*

ROACHED: Mane clipped short.

ROMAL: A braided leather thong that attaches to closed reins, is held in the right hand and can be used as a quirt. Popular in California.

RUNNING WALK: An artificial gait with diagonally opposed foot movement, where the hind foot oversteps the front foot. Characteristic of the Tennessee Walking Horse.

SACKING: To slap a horse with a sack or saddle blanket as a part of gentling and training.

SHANK: That portion of the cheek of the bit from the mouthpiece down.

SICKLE-HOCKED: Horse with a curved, crooked hock.

SIDESTEP, SIDE PASS or TRAVERSE: Lateral movement by the horse without forward or backward movement. See Figure 50.

SINGLE-FOOT: A term formerly used to designate the gait known as the *rack*.

SIRE: The male parent of a horse.

SLAB-SIDED: Flat ribbed.

SLOW GAIT: Another name for *running walk*.

SOUND: A term meaning the horse is physically fit and shows no signs of weakness or illness.

STABLE WALKING: A sign of boredom; the horse walks nervously from one side of his stall to the other.

STALLION: A mature male horse that can be used for breeding.

STARGAZER: A horse that holds his head too high and his nose out.

STRIDE: The distance from the point where a horse's foot leaves the ground to where that foot is again placed on the ground.

STUD: A place where stallions are kept for breeding.

STUD BOOK: A registry of the pedigrees of horses kept by breeding associations. A stud book lists the name and pedigree of each registered horse of the breed.

STYLISH: Having a pleasing, graceful, alert general appearance.

SURCINGLE: A broad strap about the girth of the horse.

TACK: Riding equipment or gear for the horse, such as saddle, bridle, halter, etc.

TAPADERA: Stirrup cover.

THREE-GAITED: A saddle horse trained to perform at the walk, trot and canter.

THRIFTY: Healthy, active, vigorous horse that stays in good condition without too much feed.

TREE: The wooden or plastic frame of a saddle.

TROT: A gait where the horse's legs move in diagonal pairs.

VICE: An acquired habit that is annoying or may interfere with the horse's usefulness, such as cribbing.

WALK: A slow four-beat gait where the horse always has at least two feet on the ground.

WAR BRIDLE: An emergency bridle or halter made of rope. Very severe when yanked hard.

WEANLING: A young horse during the calendar year in which it was born. On the first January 1, it becomes a yearling.

WEAVING: A sign of boredom; the horse shifts weight nervously from one foot to another, like a pendulum.

WITHERS: The ridge on a horse's back between the shoulder bones. See Figure 5.

WRANGLER: One who rounds up and saddles range horses.

YEARLING: A young horse during the first calendar year (January 1 to December 31) following the year of its birth.

Horse Colors

Here are the colors of horses as described by the American Quarter Horse Association:

BAY: Body color ranging from tan, through red, to reddish brown; mane and tail black; usually black on lower legs.

BLACK: Body color true black without light areas; mane and tail black.

BROWN: Body color brown or black with light areas at muzzle, eyes, flank, and inside upper legs; mane and tail black; usually black on lower legs.

SORREL: Body color reddish or copper-red; mane and tail usually same color as body but may be flaxen.

CHESTNUT: Body color dark red or reddish-brown; mane and tail usually same color as body but may be flaxen.

DUN: Body color yellowish or gold; mane and tail may be black, brown, red, yellow, white or mixed; often has dorsal stripe, zebra stripes on legs and transverse stripe over withers.

BUCKSKIN: A form of dun with body color yellowish or gold; mane and tail black; usually black on lower legs.

RED DUN: A form of dun with body color yellowish or flesh colored; mane and tail red.

GRULLO: Body color smoky or mouse-colored (not a mixture of black and white hairs, but with each hair mouse-colored); mane and tail black; usually black on lower legs.

PALOMINO: Body color a golden yellow; mane and tail white.

GRAY: Mixture of white and black hairs; usually born solid colored or almost solid colored and becoming lighter with age.

RED ROAN: More or less uniform mixture of white and red hairs.

BLUE ROAN: More or less uniform mixture of white and black hairs, usually with a few red hairs.

Horse Markings

The markings, usually in white, that you most frequently see on a horse:

SNIP: Any marking, usually vertical, between the two nostrils.

STAR: Any marking on the forehead.

STRIP: A long vertical marking running down the entire length of the face from forehead to nasal peak.

BLAZE: A broader, more open strip.

STAR AND STRIP: A marking on the forehead with a strip to the nasal peak. The strip does not have to be an extension of the star.

STAR, STRIP and SNIP: A marking on the forehead with a narrow extension to the nasal peak and opening up again between the nostrils.

BALD: A very broad blaze that can extend out and around the eyes and down to the upper lip and around the nostrils.

CORONET: Any narrow marking around the coronet above the hoof.

HALF PASTERN: A marking which includes only half the pastern above the coronet.

PASTERN: A marking which includes the entire pastern.

SOCK: A marking which extends around the leg from the coronet halfway up the cannon bone, or halfway to the knee on the foreleg or halfway to the hock on the hind leg.

STOCKING: A full marking almost to the knee on the foreleg and almost to the hock on the hind leg. It is an extended sock.

13.
Want More Information?

If you are anxious to learn more about horses—to become more proficient in training and riding—there are many good books, booklets, magazines and other publications that will help you.

Here are a few of the better books on Western horsemanship:

Using the American Quarter Horse, by L. N. Sikes with Bob Gray. Published in 1958 by the Saddlerock Corporation; 160 pages.

The Golden Book of Horses, by George McMillan. Published in 1968 by Golden Press; 105 pages.

The Western Horse: Its Types and Training, by John A. Gorman. Published in 1967 by Interstate Printers & Publishers; 452 pages.

The Schooling of the Western Horse, by John Richard Young. Published in 1954 by the University of Oklahoma Press; 322 pages.

Understanding and Training Horses, by A. James Ricci. Published in 1964 by J. B. Lippincott Company, 146 pages.

Training Tips for Western Riders, by L. N. Sikes and Bob Gray. Published in 1963 by the Cordovan Corporation; 60 pages.

Horses and Horsemanship, by M. E. Ensminger. New Fourth Edition, 1962, by Interstate Printers & Publishers; 921 pages.

Practical Western Training, by Dave Jones. Published in 1968 by D. Van Nostrand Co.; 176 pages.

Fundamentals of Barrel Racing, by Martha Josey. Published by the Cordovan Corporation; 96 pages.

Breaking and Training the Stock Horse, by Charles O. Williams. Published by Charles O. Williams, Hamilton, Montana; 144 pages.

Numerous booklets are available from Extension Services, feed companies, pharmaceutical companies and other sources. Here are a few excellent ones:

Horses and Horsemanship and *Horse Science,* prepared by the Federal and State Extension Services for the 4-H Horse Program. Free from county agents.

Western Horses, by John A. Gorman and Dr. J. F. Ryff, University of Wyoming. An Intermountain Regional Publication, available from the Extension Service in Western states.

Some Basic Horsemanship, by William R. Culbertson and Allen G. Richardson. Available from the Agricultural Extension Service, Colorado State University.

Light Horses, by M. E. Ensminger. USDA Farmers' Bulletin No. 2127, available from county agents.

Your 4-H Horse—Care, Management, Horsemanship, by H. B. Hedgepeth. Extension Publication No. 450, Mississippi State University.

Your 4-H Horse Project, by Dale Burnett. Miscellaneous Publication 674, available from the Agricultural Extension Service, Texas A & M University.

Beginning Western Horsemanship, Advanced Western Horsemanship, Games on Horseback and others. A series of 14 booklets, $1 to $2 each, published by the Western Horseman, Colorado Springs, Colorado.

Horse Care, by Frederick Harper. A softcover book distributed by Merck & Company for 85 cents.

The Thrill of a Horse. Published by Allied Mills, Inc., Chicago, Illinois, and free from Wayne Feeds dealers.

Selecting, Feeding and Showing Horses. Free from Albers Milling Company, Kansas City, Missouri, or Spur dealers.

The Purina Horse Book. Published by Ralston Purina Company, St. Louis, Missouri, and free from Purina dealers.

In addition to these sources, more than forty horse magazines are published in the United States. The better Western horse magazines (other than breed magazines) which contain how-to information are:

The Western Horseman
3850 North Nevada Avenue
Colorado Springs, Colorado 80901

The Horseman
5314 Bingle Road
Houston, Texas 77018

Horse & Rider
116 East Badillo Street
Covina, California 91722

Several of the horse breed associations also have literature on selecting, training and riding a horse. Here are the major breeds (in order of number of horses registered) and their association addresses:

American Quarter Horse: American Quarter Horse Association, P.O. Box 200, Amarillo, Texas 79105.

Thoroughbred: The Jockey Club, 300 Park Avenue, New York, N.Y. 10022.

Appaloosa: Appaloosa Horse Club, Box 403, Moscow, Idaho 83843.

Arabian: Arabian Horse Club Registry of America, 332 South Michigan Avenue, Chicago, Illinois 60604, and the International Arabian Horse Association, 224 E. Olive Avenue, Burbank, California, 91503.

Shetland: American Shetland Pony Club, P.O. Box 2339, West Lafayette, Indiana 47906.

American Saddle Horse: American Saddle Horse Breeders Association, 401 Wood Street, Louisville, Kentucky 40203.

Pinto-Paint: Pinto Horse Association of America, Box 3984, San Diego, California 92103, and the American Paint Horse Association,

P.O. Box 12487, Fort Worth, Texas 76116.

Welsh Pony: Welsh Pony Society of America, Inc., Unionville, Pennsylvania 19375.

Morgan: The Morgan Horse Club, Inc., P.O. Box 2157, Bishop's Corner Branch, West Hartford, Connecticut 06117.

Pony of the Americas: Pony of the Americas Club, Inc., P.O. Box 1447, Mason City, Iowa 50401.

Palomino: Palomino Horse Breeders of America, Box 249, Mineral Wells, Texas 76067, and Palomino Horse Association, Box 446, Chatsworth, California 91311.

Tennessee Walking Horse: Tennessee Walking Horse Breeders' Association of America, P.O. Box 87, Lewisburg, Tennessee 37091.

And here are some smaller breed associations:

American Buckskin Registry Association, P.O. Box 772, Anderson, California 96007.

The Spanish Mustang Registry, Inc., Box 26, Thompson Falls, Montana 59873.

American Andalusian Association, Box 1290, Silver City, New Mexico 88061.

American Connemara Pony Society, Rochester, Illinois 62563.

American Hackney Horse Society, 527 Madison Avenue, Room 725, New York, N.Y. 10022.

American Albino Association, Inc., P.O. Box 79, Crabtree, Oregon 97335.

American Mustang Association, P.O. Box 9243, Phoenix, Arizona 85020.

Chickasaw Horse Association, Inc., Love Valley, Statesville, North Carolina 28677.

Galiceno Horse Breeders Association, Inc., 708 Peoples Bank Building, Tyler, Texas 75701.

American Gotland Horse (Pony) Association, 110 East Parkway

Drive, Columbia, Missouri 65201.

American Quarter Pony Association, P.O. Box 1250, Lafayette, Indiana 47902.

Icelandic Pony Club & Registry, Inc., 56 Alles Acres, Greeley, Colorado 80631.

American Shire Horse Association, P.O. Box 421, Olympia, Washington 98501.

American Suffolk Horse Association, P.O. Box 421, Olympia, Washington 98501.

Belgian Draft Horse Corporation of America, P.O. Box 335, Wabash, Indiana 46992.

Cleveland Bay Society of America, White Post, Virginia 22663.

Clydesdale Breeders Association of the United States, Batavia, Iowa 52533.

Percheron Horse Association of America, Route 1, Belmont, Ohio 43718.

Miniature Donkey Registry of the United States, Inc., 1108 Jackson Street, Omaha, Nebraska 68102.

Index